Esther's Journey

A Holocaust Memoir

By Esther Elbaum Weingarten

Told to her daughter, Judith Elbaum Schumer

2012

Dedication

This book is dedicated to the memory of my mother, who went on the journey, and the memory of my father, who was part of her journey.

It is also dedicated to everyone in my family, so they will understand and remember Esther's journey.

Acknowledgments

I want to thank my husband Gary who kept encouraging me to write my mother's story, who scanned and edited all the photographs in this book, and who was consistent with good advice and patience. Thank you also to my daughter Rina who designed the maps and formatted the book, and my daughter Lauren who gave me wise suggestions.

A special thank you goes to Lisa Wable who designed the covers and Kopila Paudel who drafted the maps. Finally, I am grateful to my friend Andrea Scott who edited this book. As always, she had just the right touch.

PREFACE

"I want to tell you a story."

This was a sentence I often heard from my mother, Esther. When I was growing up, it might be prompted by something she saw on TV or a lengthy phone conversation with a friend. When I was an adult and she was visiting, she would sometimes walk in from another room with the request or greet me with it when I came home from work.

What were these stories about? Many were about her childhood in Poland, her parents, school friends and sisters and brothers. But most were about the Holocaust, her escape from Nazi-occupied Poland, her journey to join my father in Lithuania, and her life in China. Each time she said to me, "I want to tell you a story," I got another fragment of her experiences, usually told with many digressions, and frequently with repetitions of oft-told tales.

In the early 1990s I was helping a friend of ours, also a Holocaust survivor, write his memoir, and I realized that if I wanted to preserve my mother's story, I would have to get her to tell it from beginning to end. So, in the summer of 1994 when she was visiting me from Israel, we sat down with a tape recorder and she, once again, told me a story. And this time, I really listened.

William Maxwell, an editor of *The New Yorker* magazine, once wrote that "memory often changes with the telling." Some of the stories my mother told me at our sessions were slightly altered from earlier versions I had heard. Which were accurate? I can't be sure but everything in this memoir is as my mother last remembered it.

The stories are in her voice. Most of the time she spoke to me in English, though occasionally she explained something in Yiddish. Though I corrected my mother's grammar, the stories are as she told them.

Judith Elbaum Schumer

Poland – August 1939

CHAPTER 1

A long time ago you asked me if the war hadn't come, would our family have left Poland? Do you remember? The answer, of course, was no. Even with its long history of anti-Semitism, Poland was our home. Before the war there were more than three million Jews in Poland. Three million! We had a good life there, mostly a good life, before the war, before the Nazis came.

I was born in Minsk-Mazovyetsky, a small city about twenty-five miles east of Warsaw on the Wednesday of Chanukah, 1910. It was the Jewish calendar date that I always celebrated, not the Christian date. My father, Shlomo Brodowicz, had a lumberyard and our family was very comfortable financially. I had two sisters and two brothers, although one of my brothers died when he was just a boy.

When I was about three years old, my family moved to Warsaw for a few years. Around my fourth birthday, in 1914, I developed the mumps and my eyes became irritated and very sensitive to light. My mother asked an eye doctor, who lived in our apartment building, to come and see me. Of course, I didn't understand who he was, but the ophthalmologist who treated me that day was the world-famous Ludwig Zamenhof, the linguist who created the international language Esperanto. He is less well known today, but in Europe at that time and for many years after his death, he was a celebrity. The story about Dr. Zamenhof coming to our apartment and treating my eye problem was often retold in my family. And the street we lived on was renamed *Ulica Zamenhofa*, Zamenhof Street, a few years after his death in 1917.

We returned to Minsk-Mazovyetsky when I was still quite young. My brothers went to *cheder*, to the Jewish religious school, but in those days there were no Jewish schools for girls in my town so my sisters and I went to the public school, which in Poland meant a Catholic school. It wasn't easy being a Jewish girl in a Catholic school. There was always a comment about being a *Zhid*, the nasty Polish word for Jew. I remember one time, one of my Polish classmates answered a question incorrectly, and the teacher said to her, "You are as stupid as a Jewish horse." Since I was never able to hold my tongue, I raised my hand and asked the teacher if she could tell us the difference between a Jewish horse and a Catholic horse. The teacher wrote a letter to my father about my rude manner, and my father tried to discipline me. I was furious that he didn't take my side.

"Why should I accept remarks like that?" I asked him.

"That's just the way it is," he answered. "It's better to ignore it."

Except for incidents like that, my childhood in Minsk-Mazovyetsky was wonderful. I had many friends, both Jewish and Catholic, and I was a very good student. In the winter, when the ponds froze, we went ice-skating, and in the summer we played outdoors and went for walks in the woods.

My mother, Sarah, was a very religious woman. My father was less religious, but he still went to the synagogue on Shabbat, and we celebrated all the Jewish holidays. But in those days, girls only went to the synagogue on Rosh Hashanah and Yom Kippur, and I was more influenced by my freethinking and Zionist friends than by my religious family.

I told you that I had two brothers, Samuel and Wolf—known as Voveck. When Voveck was a boy, maybe eleven or twelve, he was walking home from *cheder* in the winter when he was attacked by some Polish boys, hooligans, who beat him, threw him into a nearby pond, and then ran away. The water was ice-cold, and Voveck was barely able to pull himself out. He ran home in his freezing wet clothing, and by the time my mother saw him, he could barely speak. The next day he became sick, and he never really recovered. I don't know exactly what his illness was—I was only about six or seven at the time—but I think he may have gotten polio. My parents went all over Poland to try to find doctors to help him, but he died in a few years. I barely remember him. I don't have his photo, but that was Poland in those days.

My father, Shlomo, died when I was twelve and my older brother, Samuel, took over the lumberyard. My mother and sisters and I continued living in our house in Minsk-Mazovyetsky and tried to get on with our lives without father. When I finished elementary school I wanted to go to high school, which then was not required by law. There were Jewish quotas in those days for the *gymnasium*, the high school, and only a small number of Jewish students were admitted each year. Fortunately, I received a very high mark on the entrance exam, and I was accepted to the school. Here, there were also some anti-Semitic teachers and students, but I learned to ignore most of the comments and I studied very hard.

When I graduated from high school, which probably was at the level of a junior college, I moved to Warsaw where one of my sisters, Sima, had moved after she got married. I got a job as a kindergarten teacher in a Jewish school, and I started dating Warsaw men, who I thought were very

Esther – Warsaw, June 4, 1932

sophisticated compared with the boys and men I knew in Minsk-Mazovyetsky. Can I tell you something? I was a bit of a flirt, though quite innocent compared with today. When I was twenty, some friends introduced me to Moshe Elbaum, to your father, who was a writer for a Yiddish newspaper in Warsaw. At that time there were many Yiddish newspapers in Poland, and it was very prestigious to be a journalist.

Just a few weeks after we started seeing each other, Moshe invited me to a very important party, a ball, where there would be many famous Yiddish actors, actresses, artists, and writers. It was winter and I bought a special gown and a fur muff for my hands. I also decided to get a permanent for my hair. Permanent waves had become very popular—they were called Marcel Waves—and they were done at the hairdresser with heated curling irons. On the morning of the ball, I went to the hairdresser and for several hours she marcelled my hair. But, she left the irons on for too long and she burned my scalp. Although my hair looked wonderful, my head felt like it was on fire. That afternoon it snowed and as I was putting on my new green gown I wondered how Moshe would be able to get me because the streets already had more than a foot of snow. When he came to the door, he was wearing a *smoking*, a tuxedo, and out on the street was a *droszka* with runners, an old-fashioned sleigh, pulled by a horse and with a driver in the front! That's how we were getting to the ball — it was like a drawing in a child's fairy-tale book! I forgot about my burning scalp and had an unforgettable evening with the man who I knew would become my husband.

Esther, Sarah, and Moshe - Warsaw, December 8, 1936

We were supposed to get married on November 20, 1932, but a few weeks before my wedding, my mother Sarah died. The rabbi who was to marry us told us that weddings should not be postponed because of a death—life needs to go on. We had a small wedding, and instead of a white dress I wore the green gown I had bought two years earlier for the ball. Moshe's two closest friends, the writers Jacob Goldstein and Moishe Nudelman, were our witnesses. Both these men survived the Holocaust, but their wives and children died in concentration camps. Years later, we resumed our friendships with them in New York.

Moshe and I moved to a very nice apartment in a mixed neighborhood in Warsaw—by mixed I mean it was Jewish and Christian. Your father had an important position at the Yiddish newspaper where he wrote and he was becoming known throughout Warsaw as a journalist who could get a story before anyone else. On November 21, 1936, your sister, Sarah, was born. I had had two miscarriages and we were both so happy to finally have a child. Moshe - I now called him Father - was just crazy about her.

In 1938 Father heard that the British Foreign Secretary, Anthony Eden, was taking a train from Germany to Moscow and that the train would stop in Warsaw for a short time at five in the morning. Father, who was one of the few writers in the city who spoke English, was the only one to go to the railroad station at that hour. When the train stopped, he went aboard and had an exclusive interview with Eden about Britain's views about Hitler and Germany and the possibility of war. He called me from the station and told me what time to listen to the radio because they would be "playing the song we like"—our prearranged code that meant he got the interview and he would broadcast what Eden had said. Then, he went to his newspaper to write the article and the paper's headline that day was "Interview with Eden." For days, both the Polish and Yiddish newspapers wrote about Moshe Elbaum's coup.

Life was good for us in Poland in those years. Our friends were writers, poets, actors and actresses—the intelligentsia in our Jewish Warsaw world. We couldn't have imagined how it would change.

CHAPTER 2

The summer of 1939 was very difficult for all of us in Poland. We knew that the Germans might invade Poland as they had invaded and annexed Czechoslovakia in 1938. Because Father was a journalist, we knew more than most people what was going on in our country and in Europe. We knew that Hitler said the Free City of Gdansk—what he called "Danzig"—really belonged to Germany and he wanted to annex it. Chamberlain, the British Prime Minister, had said that if Germany invaded Poland, England and France would be on our side and fight with us. So the feeling that war might come was all around us.

But even though there was the talk of war everywhere, and many patriotic speeches were given, life went on. In August, Father and Sarah and I went on vacation in the country near the city of Otvotsk, about seventeen miles southeast of Warsaw. On the last day of August we were supposed to go home but we couldn't locate the man who had helped us bring everything from home—besides our luggage we had Sarah's crib and toys. So we decided that I would go home by train and Father would try to find a ride home with all our things. Amazingly, he found a truck driver who agreed to take him back to the city. Father was a member of the Yiddish Writers' Union but also of the Polish Writers' Syndicate and the Syndicate had issued all its members a card that entitled them to travel anywhere in Poland for free. The truck driver was impressed with that card and loaded all our belongings onto the truck, and he and Father took off. Then Sarah and I walked to the small train station. The stationmaster told me that the trains weren't following the schedules and that he didn't know when the next train to Warsaw would arrive. We were the only two people there, and we sat down and waited. Finally, after waiting for two hours, a train arrived and at 9:30 that night we came back in Warsaw. I took a horse-taxi home— gasoline was almost impossible to get by then—and I asked the driver why there were no lights on in the houses.

"Don't you know?" he answered me. "There's a blackout. All the windows have to be covered!"

This was the moment I knew Poland was going into war.

When we came into our apartment, I saw our luggage and crib in the hallway but Father wasn't home. I learned later that he had gone to his office to find out the latest news. He also had to send cables to America because he was the Polish correspondent for the newspaper *The Jewish Daily Forward* in New York. When he came home around midnight, he told me not to worry. His colleague Aaron Singer, the government correspondent, had told him "everything will be alright!" As we know, he was wrong.

At 4 AM on September 1, Germany attacked Poland. They bombed all the Polish airplanes, they bombed factories, but they also bombed Jewish resorts, towns where many Jews lived, a Jewish orphanage outside of Warsaw, and the town of Otvotsk, where we had been the night before. Although they didn't bomb Warsaw itself the first night, the air raid sirens went off and woke all of us. We didn't know yet if it was for real or just a drill. In the morning we found out we were really at war.

On the Monday, September 4, the Polish government asked all its Writers' Syndicate members to "go east." It said that the war would be over in a week or two, and it wanted its writers to be safe. On the radio the government said that it had the fifth largest army in Europe and hundreds of tanks and an excellent cavalry—yes, it boasted about having many men on horses! We found out later the army wasn't really mobilized for war, even though the government believed war would come. The generals even complained that the Germans, unfairly, came with tanks and didn't fight like gentlemen on horses!

When Father told me that the government wanted all writers, Jews as well as Poles, to leave for the east, I told him he had to go. But he refused.

"I can't leave you and Sarah alone," he said. "I'm not leaving my wife and child while a war is going on!"

But something inside me—maybe a sixth sense—told me he had to go. I reminded him what happened to the Jewish journalists in Germany and Austria when Hitler came to power. Even in Czechoslovakia, the first victims were the journalists.

"And you belong to the Anti-Hitler Committee. You know the Nazis will arrest all the members."

"But how will you manage?" he asked me.

I pulled up the sleeves of my dress and showed him my muscles. "See? I am very strong."

We argued for a while, but I finally convinced him that he had to go. It took a few days for him to get ready to leave and I kept reminding him that if by some miracle, Poland could beat Germany, he could return.

He kept a small amount of money for himself but left me most of what he had. He also left the passbook for our Polish Savings Bank account and told me to withdraw that money as soon as I could. Now that he had

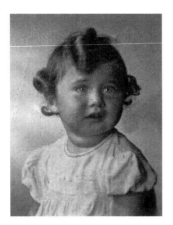 

Photos of Sarah and Esther that Moshe took with him when he left Warsaw in September 1939

agreed to go, I became agitated but I tried not to show my nervousness to him. As he was getting ready, I gave him a block of chocolate and looked around to see what else I should give him. There was a cucumber and a knife on the kitchen table and I handed both to him.

He laughed and said, "Why are you giving me the knife."

I looked at the knife and said, "You might need it if you have to fight—and maybe also to cut the cucumber." Then I, too, laughed. Otherwise, I would have cried.

It was a warm, beautiful September day, but I insisted he wear layers of clothing and his raincoat. He also took the recent photos of Sarah and me. He kissed us both at the door and he left.

I knew I had to put up a brave front for my daughter because I didn't want to frighten her, but once Father left I was very scared. Sarah was sick—she had a bad cold—and I did what I could to make her feel better. Each day there were air raids and we could hear bombs exploding in the distance. The air raids and bombing sounds terrified her and she screamed and clung to me whenever they began.

As soon as I could, I went to the bank to get our money, but there were hundreds of people there, all trying to get their money out and the bank said we couldn't get our money "at this time." Several weeks before the war started, newspapers reported that the famous Polish acting and singing couple, Marta Eggerth and Jan Kiepura, took their money out of the bank. They were criticized for being unpatriotic. As I walked home with Sarah without the money I thought that I, too, should have been "unpatriotic" and taken our money out earlier.

The next day, I left Sarah with a neighbor and walked to the Jewish Writers' Union to see if they had some news of the writers who had left the city. They said they hadn't heard from any of them yet and they would let me know if they did. But they did have some good news. The Union had withdrawn its money from the bank just before the war began, and they were dividing it among the members or their families in Warsaw. Someone, I was told, would bring me my share in a day or two.

The next day, there was a knock at my door. I asked who it was.

"Mrs. Elbaum? I am Liebel Baim, from the Writers' Union. I have something for you."

I opened the door and a man I vaguely recognized came in and told me he had some money for me. He took an envelope from his pocket and handed it to me. I asked him if he wanted some tea, but he refused.

"Thank you, but I can't stay. But I have something important to tell you. I am going to try to get out of Warsaw and across the border today with my wife and children. A peasant, a Polish peasant is going to take us."

Then he took a piece of paper out of his pocket that was torn in half.

"I wrote the man's name here. When he comes to you and shows you the other half of the paper, you'll know that you can trust him and you and your daughter can go with him. He'll try to get you across the border, too."

"I don't know what to say," I stammered. "Thank you. And I can only wish you and your family good luck in getting away from here. I'm just grateful my husband left. I hope he is safe somewhere."

We said good-bye and Liebel Baim left. That night, the Germans began an almost constant bombardment of the city of Warsaw.

CHAPTER 3

The last days of September were terrible. Bombs fell all the time, and people were taking shelter in my building because their houses had been destroyed. It was dangerous to be on the street because low-flying planes would shoot at pedestrians. The lower part of my building became a bomb shelter. During one lull in the bombing, I said that someone needed to take care of the old people, and I would take care of the children. I was the youngest adult woman there, but I was the only one who thought of organizing us. Then I took Sarah and the children and started dancing and singing with them. One of the older women twirled her fingers near her head to indicate that I was crazy, but it didn't matter. When the bombs started falling again, I sang even louder and danced faster. We all became dizzy, but it kept the children—and me—from being even more frightened.

Most of the people who lived in my building were Jewish but there were Catholic families who also lived there and with whom I was neighborly. I was shocked and hurt when one of them said, "Well, you Jews wanted Hitler—now you'll get him." Another said, "You Jews bought houses. Why didn't you buy planes for us?" The worst came from a woman who lived just across the hall from me, whom I had had to my home for tea. We had both come up the stairs and were just about to enter our apartments when she turned to me and said, "The only good that will come of all this is that the Jews will finally get their due for killing Jesus Christ." Then she closed her door. I was so stunned by her comment that I could hardly breathe. The anti-Semitism in Poland was very strong, and I wondered if the Poles would do anything to help us if and when the Nazis came in.

One day, I was sitting in my dining room with a neighbor while Sarah was sleeping in her crib. Suddenly and without warning, a bomb exploded outside on my street. The noise was intense and something shattered above me and flew past my head. I think my eardrum was torn by the noise, and I opened my mouth to scream. At that moment, for the first time, I regretted sending Father away and wished that he were there with me. The neighbor realized that I was on the verge of hysteria, and he pressed his fingers into my temples and held them there until I calmed down. Then, another bomb exploded outside and the whole building began to shake. We were afraid it would collapse so I grabbed Sarah, my neighbor went to get his family, and we and all the other people in the apartment house ran out into the street. There were fires all around—parts of the road were smashed and the buildings down the street had been badly damaged. People were running, just running, to get away. It seemed that we ran for miles. I was holding Sarah in my arms and when my neighbor wanted to take her from me, she screamed and held on to me tightly.

Finally, a group of us came to a building that had been untouched by the bombs. It was a screw factory. We went inside to see if there was a bomb shelter there. The factory had a cellar, already with many people there, but there was enough room for the group from my building. In one corner, a woman was cooking farina on a small stove, and she gave some to all the children. We stayed in that cellar until there was an all-clear siren. Then we all left and slowly walked back to see if our homes had been destroyed. We were fortunate because our building, along with a few others, was still standing, though most of the windows had been broken and some walls had huge holes. Sarah had fallen asleep in my arms on the walk back. When I went into my apartment, I saw broken glass and plaster everywhere. I cleaned off her crib and put her into it and wrapped her with many blankets. It was cold in the apartment and my daughter was still sick.

The next day, September 28, I found out that the Polish forces that had been defending Warsaw had surrendered the night before. I knew it was only a matter of days before all of Poland fell.

With almost all the windows broken, the apartment was very cold. The only room with windows still intact was the kitchen. I brought a mattress and Sarah's crib in there, and we mostly stayed in that room.

Food was not a problem yet because I had several bags of flour, farina, and kasha, and I also had tins of sardines and other food. Also, I was able to get water from the faucet and the toilet still worked. The day after Warsaw fell, my nursemaid, Basha, came back. She was a young 18-year-old Jewish girl from a very poor family who worked for me, helping me with Sarah and with the house. In those days, almost everyone in the city had someone to help with the children. Diapers had to be boiled on the stove, baby food had to be made by hand, and laundry was washed in a tub. So it seemed necessary to have help, and it cost very little since a bed and food were also provided.

Basha had gone back to her village when we went on vacation to Otvotsk in August, and she had been unable to return until now. I was overjoyed to see her and so was Sarah, but I was also concerned.

"Basha, my husband is gone, and I don't know what's going to happen now. Also, I can't pay you."

"That's alright, Mrs. Elbaum. I was so worried about you and Sarenka. I was afraid you had been hurt. I want to stay here and help you." Sarenka was Sarah's nickname—it means "little deer."

Basha had brought some food from her village. Now the three of us slept in the kitchen. While she watched Sarah, I went out and looked through the rubble to see what I could find to burn in the stove. In the past, coal was brought up to the apartment, but that was now impossible to buy. I found pieces of a wooden fence, which I somehow broke up, books, and other trash. Among the books I burned were Hitler's *Mein Kampf* and Marx's *Das Kapital.*

Sarah still had a very bad cold, and then she developed a fever that wouldn't go away. Again, Basha stayed with Sarah while I went to find a doctor for her. The doctor's office had been bombed but the doctor was unhurt, and he said he would send a nurse to see Sarah. Later that day, the nurse came to our apartment. She had no medicine, but she brought "cups" and "cupped" her back. In a few days, Sarah got better.

On October 6, Poland surrendered to the Germans. The distant bombings and gunfire stopped and it was very quiet. The first order from the Nazis, for everyone, was that there was a 7 PM curfew. We had no idea what would happen next. In the meantime, I had two unexpected visitors— one wonderful and the other frightening. The wonderful visitor was my sister, Charna, whom we called Tsesha, who was living in our home town of Minsk-Mazovyetsky and who had ridden a bicycle to come see me. She brought bread and butter and cheese—all now unavailable in Warsaw. She also had chocolates that she said some German soldiers had thrown into her basket. She looked very much like me, but with a little turned-up nose. The Germans obviously didn't think she was Jewish and only saw a beautiful young Polish woman riding her bike. It was a long and dangerous ride for her, but she wanted to know if we had survived the bombings.

"Please come back to Minsk-Mazovyetsky with me, since Moshe is gone. It will be better for you and Sarenka."

"No," I answered. "I can't go back with you. I hope to hear from Moshe soon and I will try to join him, wherever he is."

"But that will be so dangerous for you, traveling with a small child. You don't even know if he is alive."

She was right, of course. I still had had no word from him, but I told her I couldn't come back with her, not yet anyway. She stayed with me for a day, then bicycled back to Minsk-Mazovyetsky to her family. I never

Charna (Tsesha) - Esther's sister - early 1930's

saw her again.

The second unexpected visitor was a German SS officer, who loudly knocked on my door. Basha let him in, and he came into the living room where I was standing with Sarah. He looked around and tapped the handle of a leather whip against his black boot.

He saw a photo of Father on a desk and pointed to it.

"We have the name of Mozeck Elbaum on our list as a member of the Anti-Hitler Committee." He used Father's Polish name. "Where is he?"

"I don't know," I answered. "He left in early September."

He then pointed to our telephone. It was a unique white phone that had been a special gift to Father.

"I will take the telephone and the radio." He called out a name and a young German soldier who had been outside the door came in and carried out the large radio unit. Sarah began to cry and said, "He's taking our radio," which she pronounced as "yadio."

Basha picked up Sarah as the SS officer pulled out the cord from the wall and wrapped it around the white phone.

"What else do you have?" he asked.

I showed him the cracks in the ceiling made during the bombings.

"Only those," I answered, and I was immediately terrified at what I had said. But I didn't show it.

For a moment, he was silent. Then he spoke.

"*Gnädige Frau*," he said in German. "*Das is Krieg*." Dear lady, this is war. And he clicked his heels together and left.

Basha collapsed as soon as the door closed. She was nearly hysterical while holding my crying daughter.

"How could you say that?" she moaned. "He could have hit you with that whip! He could have shot all of us!"

"I just had to say something," I told her. "I just couldn't accept this indignity without a response." Then I looked down at the floor and saw that I had urinated. I had been more terrified than I realized. My mother had always warned me that I had a sharp tongue and that it might get me into trouble. But I think it also saved our lives.

Within days of that incident, the Nazis issued an order that all Jews must turn in their telephones and radios at a central location. People waited for hours on line to comply with the order. At least, I thought, I was saved from doing that by a "personal visit."

CHAPTER 4

In the middle of October, I had some wonderful news. A woman I knew from a neighboring building whose husband had left around the same time as Father brought me a message. She had gotten a letter from her husband who said he had heard that Father was alive and well in Vilna, Lithuania, which was now an independent area! She said that she was going to try to get there herself. I was elated by this news, and I knew now that I, too, would try to make that journey. I told her I would help her make a satchel for her trip and asked her to take a letter to Father.

I started making plans for my escape from Warsaw and Poland, though I still wasn't sure how I would do this with a child who wasn't quite three years old. My friends and family tried to dissuade me, but I knew I had to join my husband.

On the last day of October, a writer I had known from the Writer's Union came to my apartment. He greeted me formally and told me he had a special gift for me. In his pocket was a message and photo from Father. I cried out when I saw this and sat down to read the letter. It said, "Dress yourself and the child warmly. Things are meaningless—save your lives and we'll build our future again. Take money and cigarettes for bribes. Moshele."

The photograph had been taken in a studio. He was standing near a small table and on that table were the two photos of Sarah and me he had taken with him. My clever husband knew that I might not believe that a message was really from him, so he sent the photo as proof. On the reverse he had written,

"Wilno, 18. X - 39 —Vilna, October 18, 1939
*"To my dearest Etele and Sarenka, for her November birthday which I
remember."*

And at the bottom was an address in Bialystok and another in Vilna.

"What else do you know," I eagerly asked. "How did you get here?"

"All I know is that your husband is well and he asked me to give you this letter and photo. I have also brought messages for others."

Moshe with photos of Sarah and Esther on table - sent to Esther in Warsaw

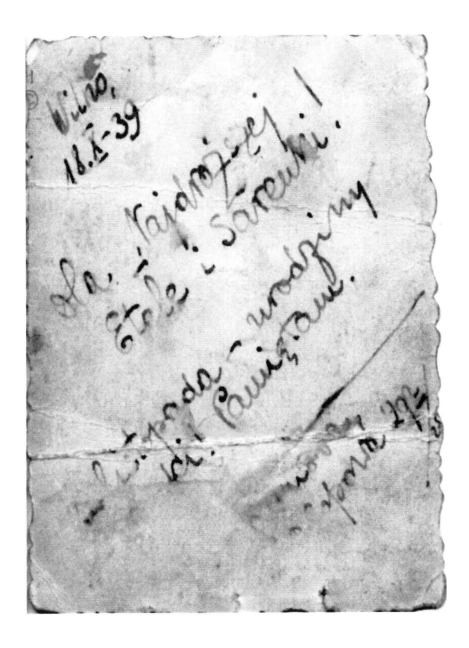

Written on the back of photo: "Wilno, 18. X – 39" —Vilna, October
18, 1939 "To my dearest Etele and Sarenka, for her November
birthday which I remember."   (Addresses no longer legible.)

Then he told me that he had taken a train from Vilna to Bialystok, but had walked from Bialystok to Warsaw. He called himself a "walker," but I think people today would call him a hiker. Before the war he would walk from town to the mountains and spend days walking around there, but in those days this was an unusual hobby. He said he had already walked back and forth to Bialystok twice, mostly at night.

I thanked him over and over again for bringing me such wonderful news and before he left he promised that if he got to Vilna before I did, he would tell my husband that Sarah and I would soon join him.

Now I really knew that I had to leave but I hadn't as yet figured out a plan. I had been visiting my cousin Rahel—her father and mine were half brothers—to discuss ways for me to safely leave Warsaw when a man approached me as I was going into my building. He addressed me in the rough Polish of a peasant.

"Are you the Elbaum woman?" he asked.

I said nothing because I didn't know what he wanted.

"If you are, I have something for you." And he took out a dirty piece of paper that was torn at the bottom. It was the upper half of the paper Leibel Baim had given me in early September and that I had almost forgotten about! The paper said, "Trust this man. On the street near the river there is now a bus that goes to the town of Sokolov. He will be on the bus and he will escort you. You will pay him then."

I couldn't believe that I was finally going to be able to leave.

"When should I be there?" I asked him.

"Tomorrow afternoon. I'll be on the two o'clock bus."

I was so excited by what this man said that I walked back to Rahel's house to tell her the news.

"How do you know you can trust him?" she asked.

"Why would he have come to me if it wasn't to help me leave Warsaw? He had the other half of that paper!"

"Just in case, I will meet you at the bus stop tomorrow."

I went back to my apartment to start getting ready. While Basha played with Sarah, I made a bundle out of a slipcover and put in the things I would need for me and Sarah. I didn't want to take a suitcase that would make it obvious that I was traveling and I could also hold a bundle more easily on my arm. I opened the lining of Sarah's small fur coat and put in my money and jewelry. I packed warm underwear for both of us and I even put in Sarah's small chamber pot. I packed whatever food I could, and the few cigarettes I had, and put many of our photos into the pockets of

Father's winter coat that I wanted to take to him. I wasn't thinking clearly, and I was sure there were things I should have taken that I didn't. I put Father's photograph from Vilna into my own coat pocket.

I was too nervous and anxious to stay in the apartment overnight. I decided to go to the home of one of my girlfriends whose mother, Mrs. Nuss, was like a second mother to me. Then I told Basha what I planned to do.

"Come with me tomorrow, Basha. We'll all get away."

"No," she replied. "I'm afraid to leave. I will go back to my parents."

I dressed Sarah and myself in several layers of clothing and the three of us left the apartment before curfew. While Basha walked down with Sarah, I locked the door to the apartment that had been my home for many years and where I had been so happy until recently. I knew that I would never be back again.

As casually as possible, not to draw attention to ourselves, we walked to the Nuss's house. My friend, whose name was also Basha, didn't know that we were coming since we both no longer had telephones, but she and her mother were so happy to see us. But I was shocked when I saw their apartment. Almost all the furniture was gone!

"What happened to your things?" I asked.

"Some Germans came in one day and took most of it. We still don't know why."

When I told my friend and her mother why I was there, they also tried to get me to change my mind.

"How can I let you go with such a small child?" Mrs. Nuss cried. "Think of what can happen? Sarenka is so precious." She knew more than anyone how precious my child was to me because she had comforted me when I had miscarried twice.

But I would not be persuaded. That night we all slept on mattresses on the floor. The next day, before I left, Mrs. Nuss gave us rolls and butter with sugar for the trip, and she and Basha hugged and kissed us. My Basha wanted to come with me, and she held the satchel while I held Sarah's hand.

About a block from the bus stop I met my cousin Rahel. Together, the four of us waited for the bus that would take me away from this city. The two o'clock bus came at half past two, but the peasant was not on the bus! I couldn't get on it because I had no idea what route the man had planned for me, so we just stood there as the bus left.

My cousin wanted me to come back with her to her house but I suddenly had an idea.

"Some buses are now running again. I am going to take any bus that is heading east. I'm ready to leave and I am leaving."

Then I had another idea.

"I have friends, the Jakuboviches, who live near the central bus station. I will see if I can spend the night with them."

Rahel looked at me and made the same twirling sign with her finger near her temple that the woman had made when I sang and danced in the bomb shelter.

"You are crazy!" she said. "Come back to my house and let's think about this."

"No," I answered. "That's what I want to do."

So the four of us walked several miles to the Jakuboviches' house. I gave Sarah a roll with butter and sugar, and she fell asleep as I carried her. Outside my friends' house Rahel hugged me and said she wished me well.

"Please try to get a message to me to let me know you are alright."

I promised and gave her a last hug.

My friend and his mother were also surprised to see me but without phones, Jews in Warsaw knew they could have unexpected visitors at any time. I told them what had happened and what I planned to do. Mrs. Jakubovich told me her husband had left in early September and that they, too, hoped to leave in a few days. She also said that she heard that tickets for the buses out of the city went on sale at midnight and that if you waited till the morning, the tickets would be sold out.

"What about the curfew?" I asked.

"The Germans don't seem to bother you in this neighborhood," my friend explained, "because the tickets now go on sale at night."

I left Basha and Sarah at the Jakuboviches' apartment and got to the bus station a few minutes before midnight. I was very surprised that a handwritten sign said that there would be a bus to Bialystok the next day. From Bialystok I would find a way to get to Vilna. The tickets were one *zloty* each and there was only one woman in the line ahead of me, but when the ticket window opened, the woman bought all the tickets for that bus! Then she turned to me and said that she was selling them for fifteen *zlotys* each! I was furious! But I had no choice—I didn't want to come here again tomorrow at midnight and take the chance that the Germans might arrest me for being out after curfew or that the bus would no longer run. So I paid her forty-five *zlotys*—fifteen each for me and Sarah and fifteen for my bundle.

Esther's Polish identity card - birth date in upper left is incorrect

The woman sneered as she took the money and gave me the three tickets.

"You Jews! How the money just runs through your fingers!"

I wanted to say something to her, to slap her, but I kept silent. I didn't want to do anything to jeopardize getting out of this city.

CHAPTER 5

The Jakuboviches were still awake when I came back from the bus station. I told them what had happened, and they agreed that I had done the right thing to pay the woman for the tickets. They went to sleep, but I was awake all night. In the morning, Basha and my friends walked me to the bus station and we all said good-bye. I hugged Basha and thanked her for all her help. She wanted to take off Father's coat that she had been wearing but I told her to keep it. It was getting cold, and she had nothing else warm to wear. In the excitement of leaving I forgot that my photographs were in the coat's pocket, and there they stayed. Everyone kissed Sarah and then we boarded the bus. It was November 7, 1939.

I went to the back, stored my pack overhead, and took a seat near the window for me and Sarah, who wanted to be on my lap. About ten adults and several older children got on. A young blond woman took the seat next to me. When the bus started, the woman whispered to me, "My name is Steffa and I'm going to Russia. My fiancé is already there and we're going to find work. I'm a Communist."

I didn't answer her and just looked out the window. Finally, I was leaving Warsaw with my daughter. We passed ruined neighborhoods, bombed and destroyed buildings, Nazi soldiers, and people searching through rubble. I couldn't wait to get away from there.

The bus moved very slowly and had to go around streets that weren't passable. Then the bus stopped at a checkpoint, and German soldiers shouted that everyone had to get off. I was terrified that they would arrest me and Sarah or send us back, but they only looked at our tickets and identity cards and searched our luggage. Then they let us go. This happened several more times and our journey was very slow. Bialystok was about one hundred miles from Warsaw, and at this rate it would take us days to get there. After several more hours the bus stopped again near a small shack and this time the driver told us our trip would continue in a large horse-drawn wagon. We all started to complain and say that we paid for a bus trip but he said he wasn't allowed to take us all the way by bus because the paved roads had been destroyed in the bombings. The wagon ride, he said, was included in our fare. Some people came out of the shack and the driver said he had to take these passengers back to Warsaw.

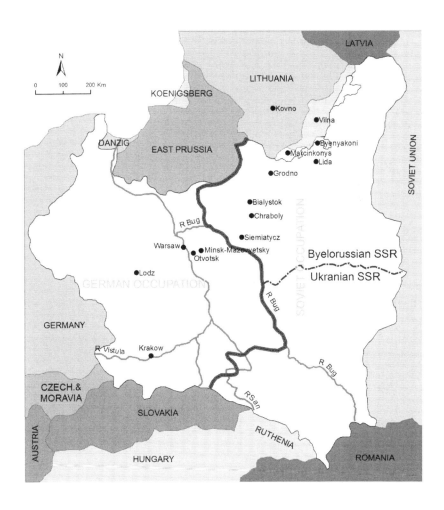

Poland and surrounding areas – November 1939

"If you want," he said, "I can take you back also."

None of us wanted to return. We piled into the wagon with our baggage, and the driver took us on a dirt road. It was dark by now, and we were all whispering about where he was taking us.

Finally, we stopped at a peasant's house. This was a kind of way station. The driver said we would spend the night here and continue on in the morning. Inside the house, the peasant's wife said we could buy supper and breakfast for a *zloty* each. I bought Sarah and me some tea and bread and dried sausage, and we went to sleep on the floor. I lay down on my bundle because I was afraid someone would steal my things, and Sarah slept on my lap. The night was filled with snores, coughs, and cries of some of the other children, and each time I fell asleep something woke me.

The next morning, the peasant woke us at about six, and we again had tea, bread, sausage, and some hard cheese. The wagon and driver were waiting outside, and we got on our way. We had only gone a few miles when the driver stopped in front of a small house and said that this was a German checkpoint and that we had to wait until the officers came.

"What time do they come?" a man asked.

"About nine," he replied and walked to the rear of the building. Steffa went over to the door and tried to open it, but it was locked. It was starting to drizzle so we all sat down with our backs to the building to try to stay as dry as we could. It was only 7 AM and we had a long wait ahead of us.

Promptly at nine, a car arrived with several German soldiers and an officer. The officer was impeccably dressed, and when he came near us I could smell his shaving cream. We all stood up, and he started looking at our papers and asking our destination. When he came over to me, I opened my mouth as if to say something, but then thought better of it and closed my mouth. The German looked at me and asked in German,

"You want to say something?"

"Well, yes," I said to him in Polish. "Why are we sitting out here when it's raining? The children are all wet and cold." I had studied German in school, but I chose to answer in my language.

The officer stared at me for a moment, then called over one of the soldiers and told him to escort all the women and children inside the building. When we were inside, the officer came over to me, looked at my identification paper, and then asked what was inside my bundle, which I had left near the door. For a moment I couldn't remember all the things I had put into it in my hurry to leave and as I hesitated, the soldier who had taken us in began to untie the bundle. I noticed that he had a bruise on his face as if he had been hit.

The German officer spoke to him harshly. "You must bring it here and open it in front of this woman." The man brought it over and I opened it. On the top was a jar of jam I had made in Otvotsk that summer. The officer opened it and smelled the jam.

"Raspberry?" he asked in German.

"Yes," I answered in Polish.

Then he took out a razor and blades I was bringing to Father.

"Why do you have these?"

I pointed to my underarm and made a shaving motion.

"Our women in Germany don't do that," he told me.

I shrugged and made a small smile. Perhaps, I thought, this German wasn't cruel.

When he took out my cigarettes, I told him to take some and asked if I could smoke.

"*Bitte schön*"—please, he said. "But our women in Germany don't smoke."

I took the cigarette from him. "But their cities weren't bombed like Warsaw was bombed."

He said nothing more to me, motioned to the soldier to close the bundle and moved on to the next woman. She began to cry as he approached her, and he searched her completely, even telling the soldier to look at the soles of her shoes to see if she had hidden something in them.

Finally, after more than two hours, the Germans let us go and we once again got onto the wagon. I gave Sarah some bread and cheese that I had saved from that morning, and we bumped along the road. But again, after a few hours, the wagon stopped at a guard station, and the wagon driver told us to get out.

"Why are we stopping now?" asked one of the men.

"This is as far as I go," said the driver. "The River Bug is a mile or so down the road. You all can walk there and the boat will take you across."

Everyone started shouting at once and telling the driver that he had been paid to take us all the way. Sarah started to cry and I tried to comfort her while also yelling at the driver. Then a soldier from the guard station came over to us and asked what was going on.

"This driver," I said to the young man in the German uniform, "was paid to take us all the way and now he refuses to take us to the river. He says we have to walk. How can I walk there with my small child and my bundle? It's the same for the others."

The soldier looked at Sarah who was still crying and said to her in Polish, "Don't cry, little girl. I have something for you."

He reached into his pocket, took out an apple, and gave it to her. I realized from his heavy accent that he was from Silesia, an area of Germany that had a large Polish population and that he was probably a Pole, not a German. Sarah took the apple and said, "*Tze tze tze*…Give us back our radio and telephone." His uniform made her think he was the German who had been in our apartment.

"What did she say?" he asked, since he didn't understand her.

"It was her way of saying 'thank you.' She doesn't speak well yet."

He smiled at her, took her little fingers and kissed them. Then he turned to the driver and told him he had to take us the rest of the way. As we slowly moved down the road in the wagon, the young soldier followed us on foot. Finally, we got to a riverbank, and there was a boy of about twenty with an old rowboat standing there.

"This is not possible!" one of the women shouted. "We paid for a bus ride to Bialystok. Then we have to ride in a wagon and now this boat? We will all drown!"

Some of the others started shouting, too, and I was thinking that if the situation weren't so serious it would be like a comedy. Yesterday, when I said good-bye to my friends I never would have believed that today I would be at the edge of the River Bug, ready to cross it in a tiny boat.

"We're not going!" a few people were saying. "Take us back! Make him take us back," they said to the soldier.

The soldier started arguing with the driver, and he finally agreed to drive whoever wanted to return to a nearby village, if they paid him.

But Steffa and I and another man and woman said we wanted to continue across, to try to get to Bialystok. The boy at the rowboat heard all this and told us we had to pay him to get across and we agreed to pay him a *zloty* each.

"But the boat is small," he said. "I can only take one or two of you over at a time."

I told him that I wanted to go first with Sarah and Steffa but when he saw my pack, he said that Steffa wouldn't fit. Sarah and I had to go over alone with him.

I paid him three *zlotys*—he insisted that I pay him for my bundle—and I was too tired and nervous to argue. He started to row the boat slowly across the river. It was getting colder and as we got to the middle of the river, a wind began to blow. Then he stopped rowing.

"What's the matter," I asked.

The boy looked at us.

"I want more money," he said.

"I have no more to give you."

"I think you do. You have to give me some more."

I was silent for a few seconds. Then I said to him, "Do you believe in God?"

"Of course," he replied.

"Do you believe in Jesus and Mary and Joseph?"

"Yes, of course."

"Then when you die, and you meet them all, you will have to tell them why you have blood on your hands, why you murdered me and this child!"

"I'm not going to murder you," he almost shouted.

"Yes, you are. I told you I have no more money. So you either have to take us across, or throw us both in the river."

Sarah started to cry. "No, I don't want to go into the river."

The boy picked up the oars and continued rowing. He didn't say another word. When we got to the other side, he helped us out of the boat and put my bundle on the shore. Then he handed me back my three *zlotys*.

"You are one smart Jewess," he yelled, as he began to row back across.

CHAPTER 6

I waited on the shore until Steffa and the two others arrived in the rowboat. We had expected a wagon to be there to take us further but there was no one there. We walked away from the river to where the woods began and decided to stay there overnight. It was getting dark, and we had no idea where to go from here.

Suddenly, from a distance, we heard someone say in Hebrew, "*Shma Yisroel, Adonai Elohainu…*"

I didn't know if I heard a Jew reciting the evening prayer or praying because he was being thrown in the river. Steffa ran over to where we had heard him and came back to tell us that there were three men there, also hoping to get to Bialystok. They had paid for a man to guide them further, but he never arrived. We walked over and joined them at the edge of the forest.

Night came. I sat leaning against a tree with Sarah, and we ate some of our leftover food, including the raspberry jam from the summer. Soon we both slept. In the middle of the night we were awakened by some animal sounds, and Sarah was very frightened. To calm her, I told her to look up at the sky. High above the river we could see thousands of stars and I showed her the Milky Way.

"Is there really milk there?" she asked.

"No, just many, many stars."

My daughter and I sat there on the ground and looked up at the beautiful sky. I had never seen it look like this—the night was absolutely clear and we were covered by the canopy of glittering stars. Then I started humming Schumann's *Traumerei*—the dream song—and soon Sarah was asleep.

Dawn came and we all woke up and discussed where we should go next. One of the men who had come the day before said that there was a road about a half mile through the woods and that we should go there and start walking. He thought there was a small town nearby. We knew we couldn't just stay where we were, so we began to walk towards the road. Because it was early November, there was frost on the ground and soon my feet were very cold. I carried Sarah as well as my bundle because I didn't want her to be cold.

When we got to the road, I asked the man who was leading if he knew where we were.

"I'm not sure," he replied, "but let's walk left—I think that's towards Bialystok."

Within minutes after we started walking, a wagon and a car came towards us. There were two Polish peasants in the wagon and three soldiers in the car. They both stopped on the road in front of our group and the soldiers came out. I immediately saw that these were not Germans. They wore Russian uniforms! We had reached the area of Poland that, just before the war, Hitler had agreed the Russians could control.

"What are you doing here?" shouted one of the soldiers in Russian, as he got out of the car.

"We're just going to a nearby town," answered the woman who had come on the rowboat after me.

"No," yelled the soldier. "You *Zhids* have to go back where you came from, to your side of Poland."

He turned to one of the peasants and told him to get someone with a raft to take us all back across the river.

"And make the *Zhids* pay you!" he laughed.

My Russian wasn't very good, but I knew what he was saying and I began to shout at the peasants in Polish.

"What? Do you want to help the enemies of Poland? You will never take us back alive. You will have to let the Russians here shoot us."

Steffa and the others started to say "shh" to me, to make me stop talking like this, but I continued.

"You cannot even think about sending us back to the people who have destroyed our country. You call yourselves Poles? Shame on you!"

Then I turned to the soldier and said to him half in Russian, half in Polish.

"Sir, you have to take us to someone in authority. You cannot make such a decision. I insist you take us to your commander."

The soldier burst out laughing and then said something to his comrades in Russian that I didn't understand. They also started to laugh and got back in the car. Then the soldier spoke in broken Polish to my group.

"Get in the wagon, all of you *Zhids*. Your Polacks will follow me."

So my group of eight crowded into the small horse-drawn wagon, and we followed the car back up the road it had come from. One of the Polish men turned to us from his bench in the front and spit on the floorboard near us.

"Heh! Good luck to you *Zhids*! I can tell you these Russians aren't much better than the Germans. You'll see. Heh, heh!" He slapped his friend on the back and laughed. I saw that he had no front teeth.

We were all quiet. Sarah held on to my hand tightly and, once again, we were bumping along in a wagon, not knowing where we were headed.

We arrived at a small building with the Russian hammer and sickle flag flying from the roof. We got out of the wagon as the three soldiers went in and came out with a Russian captain. The soldier who had spoken to us pointed at me and spoke quickly to the officer. Then the officer came over to where I was standing. He was about forty years old and had a patch over one eye.

"My man over there," he said in excellent Polish, "says you and your friends here came across the Bug and that you insisted on seeing me. Is that correct?

"Yes," I answered him. "I always want to see the person in charge."

"You sound like a cultured person. There is a war going on, and yet you are walking at the border like this." He gestured with his hand slowly back and forth.

"You have a small child," he went on, "yet you come across here in such a cavalier way?"

"Oh yes," I said to him, "Of course I know there is a war. But you see, in Warsaw where I come from, we no longer have radios and newspapers, so we must rely on others for news and information. I was told that November 7 was the Russian *prazdnik*," I used the Russian word for holiday, "the day you call 'October Revolution Day' and for the days around the holiday you open the gates of your Motherland and everyone can cross."

I will never forget what happened next. The Russian looked at me with his one eye, wagged his finger at me and said in Russian, *"Toht ostraumnaya"* —Sharp thinking!

The sound of his words was like beautiful music to my ears!

"Tell me, where are you going?" he asked.

I decided that I would be truthful with this man.

"I don't know about the others, but I want to go to Vilna."

"Ah," he said, "don't say 'Vilna!' Vilna is not Russian anymore. It's the capital of free Lithuania. Be quiet about your destination."

"Alright, how about if I say 'Bialystok'? Can you help us get there?"

"Yes. I will have the wagon driver you came with take you to the village. There is a woman there who lets people stay in her house if you pay her. But tomorrow morning, I want you out of my district."

All my courage came back to me at this moment.

"Captain, you are so nice to us. Can you give us a *propusk* to help us go where we need to go?" I knew that *propusk* was Russian for a 'permit to pass.'

"If I give you that, my superiors will—" he made a slicing motion with his fingers across his neck. "And remember—don't say you are going to Vilna."

Again, our group piled into the wagon, and this time the two Poles were silent as they took us into the village and dropped us off at a small, very rough-looking house. A woman came out. The driver told her who we were and that we would pay her to stay overnight.

The woman, who was a widow, had three children. Inside the house were two rooms and very little furniture.

"The children and I will sleep on the floor tonight. You can have the beds."

She pulled out a drawer from under one of the beds and showed the men that they would sleep there. She gave Steffa and the woman a mattress in a corner. Then she took me and Sarah into the small other room where her bed was.

"You and the child will be more comfortable here. I will be on the floor."

I thanked her and told her that I would pay her for her kindness.

There was wood for the stove, but the house was very dark when evening came. It was depressing in the small, chilly house.

"Can you light the lamps?" Steffa asked her.

"I'm sorry," the woman answered her. "I have no money for kerosene."

I took out a *zloty* from my pocket and gave it to her.

"Is there somewhere you can buy kerosene now?"

She handed the money to her son and he went out to get the kerosene. When he returned and the lamps were lit, it cheered us all. The woman began peeling potatoes and for dinner that night she served us boiled potatoes with melted pork fat on top. Although I hadn't kept a kosher home, I had never eaten pork fat before. This was the first cooked food I had eaten since I had left Warsaw three days before, and it tasted wonderful.

After dinner, the woman turned off the lamps—the kerosene was too precious to waste—and we all went to bed. The woman went into the other room with Sarah and me, lit a tiny remnant of a candle, and helped me get Sarah ready to sleep. She put a blanket on the floor and lay down next to me. She quietly asked me where I was from and after I answered her truthfully, she told me about herself. She said her husband died a few years ago and that she was very poor. Her children, she said, had never gone to school. She also said that she had heart palpitations—but she had no money for a doctor or medicine.

I got out of the bed and went to my pack. It was too dark to see anything in there but I rummaged around with my fingers until I felt a small bottle.

"This is valerian. I brought it with me from Warsaw. Please take it. When your heart beats too fast take a few drops and it will help you."

The woman thanked me again and again. Just then, Sarah began to cry. She came over to me and whispered into my ear.

"Why is the poor child crying?" the woman asked.

"I'm sorry," I said to her. "My daughter says the sheet is rough against her skin. It's nothing. She'll be fine." The fabric was very coarse and was probably homemade.

The woman got up from the floor and opened a trunk at the foot of her bed. She took out a tablecloth.

"Let's put this on the bed under your child. I use it at Christmas and Easter on the table. She'll be more comfortable."

I started to protest, but she was already putting it over the sheet. Sarah lay down on it and soon fell asleep. The woman and I talked for a while longer, the candle flickered out, and soon we both slept. It was the best sleep I had in a long, long time.

Early the next morning, we all got ready to leave. The woman gave us more boiled potatoes and bread, and I shared the last of my raspberry jam with everyone, including the woman and her children. I also gave the children some hard candies I had taken with me and the rest of my sugar. When I went into the room to get my bundle, I started giving the woman some money, but she refused to take it.

"No, you have been so nice to me and my children. I won't take more money from you. You may need it."

But when she told the others how much to pay her, one of the men tried to bargain with her. I became so angry with him, and my sharp tongue went into action.

"Pay her what she wants or I will slap you! She took you in and gave you a bed and food. How dare you try to give her less!"

The man started to say something, but the others told him to be quiet. They all paid her and at the door, she motioned to a neighbor's house.

"Wait here. I will knock on his door. He has a horse and cart and if you pay him, he will take you to Siemiatycze, which has a train station. Maybe you can get your train to Bialystok there."

As we walked out of her house, she handed a piece of bread to Sarah and then leaned down her front step, picked the last of the autumn wildflowers, and also gave them to her.

"For your trip," she said. "So you will have a smile."

Sarah said thank you to her and held the bread and flowers in her little fist.

"I will save them for *tata*, she said, using her word for *tateh*—father in Yiddish. This entire journey I kept telling her that we were going to find her beloved *tata*.

The woman went over to her neighbor and told him what we wanted and that we would pay him. He agreed, but his cart could only take a few of us at a time. The woman told the others that Sarah and I had to go first. I insisted that Steffa had to come with me, and we squeezed into the cart with our bundles. The road he took was very narrow, and there were places where the branches of the trees scraped against us. I started to sing to Sarah, but the man told me to stop.

"Please stop singing. There are bandits in these forests and I don't want them to hear us. You must be quiet."

We rode to Siemiatycze in complete silence and got to the station about eight in the morning. I paid the driver and he went back for the others.

The platform was crowded with people. Soon after we got there, I saw a couple I knew from Warsaw—Mr. and Mrs. Elkis. We greeted each other like long-lost friends.

"Where are you going?" I asked them.

"We're going back to Warsaw," Elkis said to me.

"Are you crazy?" I asked him. "Warsaw is under complete Nazi occupation! Why don't you go to Bialystok, where I am going?"

"No, Mrs. Elbaum," he said. "You are the one who is crazy. You don't know what it's like there. It's full of refugees like you, but there is nothing to eat and nowhere to sleep. The Russians are all over, and I think they are as bad as the Germans."

I had no energy to argue with him, but I thought about the Captain who had helped us yesterday and decided I'd rather take my chances with the Russians.

Steffa and I sat down to wait for the train. I saw the cart bring the rest of the people from my group. In the early evening, a train to Bialystok finally came. I said goodbye to the Elkises, who were still waiting for a train going in the other direction. I thought about my terrible journey from Warsaw and wondered if they would ever get there.

The distance to Bialystok was about fifty miles, but the train stopped many times, once for a few hours, and we didn't get there until seven the next morning. It was raining when we arrived. At the station, Steffa said good-bye to me. She said that a friend from the Communist club she belonged to would help her get to her fiancé in Russia. I ran across the road to where I saw horse-taxis waiting, and once again I met someone I knew, Mordche Tzanin, a casual acquaintance of ours. He immediately told me that Father was no longer in Bialystok.

"I know," I told him. "He's in Vilna, where I want to go. But he gave me an address where I should stay while I am here."

When I told Tzanin the address, he said he knew the people.

"Their name is Goldman—they are Bundists. I think your husband stayed with them when he was here. Let me help you." The Jewish Bund was a very left-leaning organization.

Tzanin tried to take Sarah from me, and she screamed, thinking he was taking her away from me and she scratched his face. I held Sarah and gave Tzanin my bundle. He took me over to one of the horse-taxis and gave the driver the address. Sarah buried her face in my shoulder as we began our ride to our next destination. We were both wet and very, very weary of traveling.

CHAPTER 7

The Goldmans lived on the top floor of an old apartment building. When I rang the bell, Mr. Goldman came down and I told him who I was.

"You made it here from Warsaw! We thought the border was closed. Your husband got a message to us that you might come, but we didn't think you and the child would be able to get here. Come in, come in!"

The Goldmans lived there with their three-year-old son and Mrs. Goldman's mother. Mrs. Goldman welcomed us and offered Sarah and me tea and bread, but the grandmother seemed angry that we were there. I was sure she resented having to share their food with strangers, and though I understood her feelings, I felt uncomfortable being there. Sarah, though, was delighted to be with another child and was happy to play with his toys. The little boy liked Sarah and started hugging and kissing her. When she tried to pull away, he bit her arm. The grandmother slapped him and yelled at him, and though I told her he was just excited and that Sarah was alright, she pulled him away to the next room and kept yelling at him. The parents went after them, and there was more yelling.

We slept in the living room that night and early the next morning, though it was very cold, I told the Goldmans that I was taking Sarah out to see the city. I just needed to get away from the tense atmosphere in that apartment. Sarah took the piece of bread and flowers that the woman had given her the day before. She said she wanted to hold them in case we met *tata* on our walk. She kept those in her hand every day, the hardening bread and the wilting flowers, for almost month.

We started walking on the streets of the city. There were hundreds of people already out—most were refugees like me—but because Bialystok was now under Russian control, the city felt safer than Warsaw.

We kept walking. Around lunchtime, we went into a small café, but they had almost no food. I bought bitter coffee for me and tea for Sarah and some stale biscuits. As we were leaving the café, I heard someone call my name. I turned around and there was Mr. Jakubovich, my friend's father! I told him I had stayed with his wife and son the night before I left Warsaw. He told me that he hoped they would soon be able to join him here. Then I asked him if he knew someone who might want to buy my wedding ring and other jewelry.

"I am running out of money, and I want to pay the people I am staying with."

"Don't sell your ring, my dear," he said. "I can help you."

He took out his wallet and gave me half his *zlotys*. When I protested, he said he had been able to take a lot of money with him and that I could pay him back some day.

Sarah and I stayed at the Goldmans from November 11 until December 3. During that time, I met other Warsaw friends who had been able to get to Bialystok, including Goldstein and Nudelman, the writers who had been the witnesses at my wedding, the Yiddish comedic duo Dzigan and Schumacher, and the Yiddish actress Shoshana Kahan. I kept trying to find a way to get out of Bialystok. The problem was that because the city was under Russian occupation—the Russians considered it "liberation"—I would have to cross both the Russian and Lithuanian borders without a visa or valid passport. Towards the end of November, around the time of Sarah's third birthday and my wedding anniversary, I couldn't stand living with the Goldmans any more and I decided to take a chance and try to leave. The Goldmans gave me an address of a Bundist they knew in Grodno, which, like Bialystok, was now part of Byelorussia and under Soviet control. From there, I was determined to find a way to smuggle myself and Sarah into Lithuania.

On the train to Grodno, we sat next to a young Polish man who was wearing a coat with a fur collar. Sarah was fascinated by the collar and several times reached over and touched it. The man was very friendly and tickled Sarah each time she touched the collar, and she giggled with him. We started to talk and he confessed to me that he smuggled money for people in the lining of his coat. He said he traveled back and forth between Grodno, Bialystok, and Warsaw and that he was making quite a bit of money doing that.

"I hope to get back to Warsaw in a week or so. Do you want me to bring back any letters?"

I was overjoyed that I would be able to get some news about me and Sarah back to Warsaw. He gave me a pen and a paper and I wrote a letter to Mrs. Nuss and asked her to tell my family that Sarah and I were alive and on our way to Vilna. Years later, I found out that he had indeed delivered the letter to her and that she had let my family know where we were.

"I don't know if I can pay you," I said. I had very little money left and I needed it to get to Vilna.

"Don't be silly," the young man said, "I don't want any money from you. It's a favor to a lovely woman with a lovely child."

The distance to Grodno was about fifty miles, and this time, the train didn't stop on the way. When I got to the station, I found a horse-taxi and told the driver to take me to the town of Marcinkonys, which I was told was the last Russian-controlled town on the border with Lithuania. I'm not sure what chutzpah, what nerve, made me think I would be allowed to get across with my daughter, but I wanted to try.

The driver told me it was thirty-five miles to Marcinkonys and asked me why I wanted to go there.

"I have a friend in the town."

The driver snorted.

"You want to get across the border, don't you? The Russians won't let you, but it's your money, if you want to try. But you have to pay me first."

I paid him what he asked for, and we rode to the border town. I hoped my luck and sharp tongue would help me get across. This time I was wrong.

When we got to Marcinkonys, there were Russian soldiers everywhere. I told the driver to wait there, in case I had to return. He snorted again and told me that I would have to pay him if I wanted to go back to Grodno.

At the border checkpoint, I waited in line with others who wanted to cross. When it was my turn, the guard asked me for my passport. I showed him my Polish identification and said I only wanted to go across for a short time to visit a friend.

"It's my daughter's birthday," I told him, which was true. It was November 21.

"I don't care what day it is," he told me. "Without proper papers, you're not getting across."

So Sarah and I went back to the horse-taxi. The driver was leaning against the buggy and was smoking a cigarette.

"I told you wouldn't get across. But it's good for me because you have to pay me again."

This time he charged me even more than he had the first time, but I was exhausted and didn't argue with him. I gave him the money, and we went back to Grodno.

I told him the address of the Bundists who were friends of the Goldmans, and I spent the night with a very nice family. The next day, Sarah and I took a train back to Bialystok and we again went to the Goldmans. I no longer knew what to do.

On November 27, I received a telegram from Father, delivered to the Goldmans. Father knew I was there! The telegram said only a few words: "Wait. Someone will come to get you." I found out later that Tzanin, the man I had met near the Bialystok railroad station, had gotten to Vilna and found Father and told him that Sarah and I were in Bialystok, at the Goldmans.

I was so excited and happy. Somehow, I was going to get to Vilna.

On December 1, a Jewish woman dressed as a peasant came to the Goldmans. She had a lot of money for me hidden in the lining of her coat and a letter from Father telling me what to do. He said that a Polish woman, a peasant, would come on December 3 to take me to Vilna. I was to get cigarettes to use as bribes and I was to dress as warmly as I could because it was getting very cold. He also said that I should find the actress Shoshana Kahan, if I could, and take her with me. He didn't know that I knew exactly where she was.

I spent the next days anxiously waiting to leave. I said goodbye to Goldstein and Nudelman and told them I hoped we'd meet again one day. I also told Shoshana to come to the Goldmans early in the morning of December 3.

That morning, it was snowing. When Shoshana arrived, I was afraid we'd be disappointed and our guide wouldn't come. But at nine o'clock, a Polish woman arrived at the building. I said good-bye to the Goldmans, thanked them for everything, and we were on our way.

The woman took the three of us to the train station and said she had already bought tickets for us to Byenyakoni, a border town one hundred and twenty-five miles from Bialystok. At the station, we met a woman named Fella Newman, who was Tzanin's girlfriend, and three men who had also paid this woman to help them get to Vilna.

"This train will stop in Lida," she told us, "but we all will remain on till we reach the end."

"How will you get us across the border?" I inquired of her. I remembered trying to get across less than two weeks ago, but being turned back.

The woman made a face and shrugged her shoulders.

"I have a way," she answered.

I wasn't assured by her response, but I was so eager to get going. We waited for the train. When it finally arrived, I remained very anxious. Sarah soon fell asleep on my lap, still holding the dried piece of bread and the wilted flowers for *tata*.

CHAPTER 8

I sometimes still dream about my journey from Warsaw to Vilna. In my dream, wherever I try to go, someone stops me and says I cannot go that way. I go forward in one direction, then I have to go back and start again. When I think about how it really happened, it was very much like my dream.

When we left Bialystok on December 3, I hoped I would get to Father in Vilna the next day. It didn't happen like that.

The trip to Byenyakoni took many hours. When we finally arrived there and got off the train, a Russian officer came over to us and asked to see our papers.

"Where are you going?" he barked at us.

The woman who was our guide started speaking to him in Russian. He started shouting at her, and I understood him clearly when he said that we couldn't go any further. Then he showed us his identity card—he was with the NKVD, the Soviet secret police! I almost fainted from disappointment and fear.

"I am arresting all of you," he said. "You know you shouldn't be here. You have to take the next train back to Lida."

We are all tired, cold, and miserable. Sarah started to cry and I felt like crying, too. I think that that was the lowest point for me. When we had gotten on the train in Bialystok I had hoped that I was finally going to get to Father, and I had let myself believe it was true. Now, I didn't know what would happen to me and to my little daughter.

We waited for a train going in the opposite direction. When it arrived, the NKVD officer got on it with us. When we came to Lida, he told everyone except Sarah and me to go with one of the soldiers and told us to stay where we were, in front of the station. A young soldier with a rifle stood guard over the two of us. And there we stood, for nearly an hour, as the snow began to fall. Suddenly, my anger came back and I said to myself that at this point, I had nothing to lose. I started shouting.

"Why do we have to stay here in the cold? It is snowing and my child is freezing! I thought Russia was supposed to take care of children, that it was a paradise for children! This is how you treat mothers?"

The soldier with the rifle stood motionless and just looked at me but the NKVD officer came out of the station.

"What's going on here?" he yelled at me.

"I thought Russia was good to women and children and took care of people! Isn't that what Marxism teaches? I have a tired, hungry little girl here! And I am hungry and cold, too!"

He looked at me and nodded.

"Come with me," he said.

He took us both into the train station and told us to follow him upstairs. We went into a room where a railroad worker was sleeping on a cot.

"Get up," he shouted at the man, who jumped up, grabbed his coat, and ran out of the room.

"You can stay here with the child."

"We are both hungry—we haven't eaten since this morning," I told him.

The Russian looked at me and smiled. Then he said *"ladna."* I thought he was flirting with me because in Polish, *ladna* means pretty. Later, I learned that in Russian it means well or alright.

"You can go downstairs and buy something to eat for you and the girl."

"But I have no money," I told him. "The woman who is our guide was paid to get us food."

He took out 30 rubles from his pocket.

"Here. Go down and buy something to eat."

I picked up Sarah and went out of the room with the officer. He went into a small office on the other side of the landing. I went downstairs. A woman at a food kiosk told me she had nothing left but tea without sugar, so I went back upstairs to the office.

"Here is your money back," I angrily said to the Russian. "There's nothing down there but bitter tea."

I thrust the rubles into his hand.

"Wait in the other room," he said to me, as he got up and left the office.

In about twenty minutes, he came back with some sausage and bread and some candy for Sarah.

"You stay here with the child," he said. "The others will be coming here in awhile."

After he left, Sarah and I ate the food and I lay down on the cot with her. About an hour later, the NKVD officer brought Shoshana Kahan and the others, including our guide, into the room. The young soldier was told to stay with us.

"You'll sleep here tonight," the officer told us. Then he turned to the group now seated on the floor.

"And don't make too much noise. This child has to sleep. Russia is good to children."

Then he left the room.

It was a very strange night. Nine people, including the guard, were crowded into this little room. Shoshana told me that while I was outside with Sarah, the officer had gone through their belongings and had taken everything of value, including the gold watch and ring she had hidden in her hem. He had made our Polish guide search her. One man had some salt and sugar in his pack. The Russian had mixed them together, and while laughing, told him it was easier to carry that way.

I started to sing to Sarah and soon she fell asleep. Shoshana and Fella Newman and I whispered to one another in Yiddish, wondering again and again, what would happen to us tomorrow, where we would be sent. The night seemed endless.

At four o'clock the next morning, the officer came into our room and looked at my bundle.

"What do you have inside?" he asked me.

"If you think I have valuables inside," I answered him, "you are mistaken. I have our clothes and my daughter's chamber pot. You can look."

He laughed and said *"ladna"* again. I still misunderstood what he meant.

"You can all leave," he said, "except you." He pointed to our guide. "Downstairs there is an old clock on the wall. It is two hours fast. When it says seven, it will really be five o'clock. All of you go downstairs and wait. Take the seven o'clock train to Byenyakoni. Remember—seven by that clock."

We were all confused—sleepy, hungry, frightened, and confused. Why was he letting us go? One of the men said that this must be a trick, that we were going to be sent to a Russian labor camp. We went downstairs and sat on the benches to wait for the train. An old woman was selling tea at the kiosk, and we were all glad to have something warm to drink. While we were waiting, our Polish guide gave me a slip of paper.

"When you get to Byenyakoni, this is who you need to see."

The paper said *Faiga Pochter*.

"Her brother is the watchmaker there. Look for them—there's only one watchmaker in the town."

"What will happen to you?" I asked her.

"Oh, don't worry about me. They know me around here. I will be alright."

"Why are they letting us go?" I inquired. "Some of the others think we'll be sent to a labor camp."

She laughed and rubbed her thumb against her two fingers.

"That NKVD man—he got what he wanted. And I also gave him some money. You're not valuable to him anymore. Even Communists take bribes—they are no more honest than the rest of us!"

But I was not assured by her words. I left Sarah with Shoshana and went over to the Russian officer who was standing near the door.

"Sir, what is going to happen to us in Byenyakoni? Will we be arrested again?"

"When you get off the train, do as I say. Walk straight into the town. Don't go left, don't go right, don't run. Just walk to the town. You won't be arrested."

"Why don't you give me a *propusk*," I asked him, "so I can be safe?"

He gave me the same answer the other Russian officer had given me when I had asked for a "permit to pass."

"If I do that, it will be the end for me."

He made that same slicing motion across his neck.

At exactly seven by the station clock—that is, five in the morning—the train arrived at the Lida station. The NKVD officer told the men in our group to help the women with their things and once again, we got on the train to Byenyakoni. Sarah asked me if we were going to see *tata*, and I told her we were. I hoped it was true, but I was no longer sure. I felt as if we had been traveling for years. Sarah still held her two little gifts for Father.

Our exhausted group arrived in Byenyakoni at six in the morning. When we got off the train and started walking towards the town, three border guards came over to us and asked us where we were going. I became the spokesperson for the group.

"We're all going to visit my aunt Faiga Pochter. It's her birthday."

As I was speaking, an old woman dressed in black passed by and listened to what I was saying. Then she spoke to the guards in Russian.

"Pravilno. Zhivyot takaya." — Correct. Such a person lives here.

One of the guards asked the woman something in Russian and then made a motion to us to continue on. My heart was beating so hard I could hardly breathe, but I was determined not to show my fear. I held Sarah's hand tightly and looked straight ahead as we walked on the dirt road that led to the small town.

As we came to the edge of the town, we saw a tavern. A man was lighting a kerosene lamp on its porch.

"Are you open?" Shoshana shouted at him.

"Yes," he answered. "You can come in."

We wearily sat down on the benches around a rough wooden table and ordered some food and hot tea. A waitress brought sausages and bread and hard-boiled eggs—I hadn't eaten an egg since my summer vacation in Otvotsk, a lifetime ago—and hot farina for Sarah. After we ate, the men said Sarah and I should stay at the tavern with the luggage and the rest of them would go out to find Faiga Pochter and her brother. They returned a short time later and told me they found the watchmaker—a painted watch was over the door of his shop—and that we were all to go to the house behind his store.

Faiga Pochter did indeed live in the house behind her brother's shop, together with her husband and two sons. Father had heard about her from others who had been smuggled across the border and had gotten money to her so she would help us. Bribes paid to the right people still made it possible to get into Lithuania.

Later that day, three peasants arrived to take our group across the border. But Faiga said that Sarah and I had to stay.

"I was paid for you and the child to go in a wagon. The others will walk but you will ride."

"When will that wagon come?" I asked her.

"Tomorrow morning. You will stay with me tonight."

Shoshana said that she refused to go and wanted to stay with me and Sarah.

"I don't want to go without you," she insisted. "How can I leave you here alone, not knowing what will happen?"

"She'll be safe," Faiga said to her, "and I don't have room for anyone else to sleep here. You have to go now, or they won't be able to take you across."

I hugged Shoshana and told her that I believed the woman. Father had arranged for my safe passage and I trusted him.

"I'll see you in Vilna," I said to her. "Tell Moshele, if you see him, that we are coming."

When the group left, Faiga asked me if there was anything she could do for me and Sarah.

"Is there any way could clean ourselves? We haven't washed in three days."

Faiga had no indoor plumbing but she sent her sons out to get water and she heated it on her stove. I bathed Sarah in a metal tub in the middle of the kitchen. Sarah laughed as she splashed in the warm water, and for a few minutes it felt like a normal life—a mother washing her child. I used the same water to clean myself, and I felt refreshed and relaxed. Soon, I believed, I would see Father again.

That night, I ate dinner with this family, and later the boys taught Sarah some Russian songs. As I went to sleep in a bed with Sarah, I felt optimistic.

At dawn the next morning, the three peasants who had taken the group across came to Faiga's house.

"What's going on?" I asked. "Where are the others?"

"We got them across the border," one of the men answered, "and took them to a train going to Vilna. But the Russians have tightened the security—there are lots more soldiers there today. We'll have to go another way with you."

"But what about the wagon my husband paid for?" I turned to Faiga. "Didn't you say he paid you for a wagon and driver for me and my child?"

"He can't come," the man answered quickly. "It's too dangerous to take the road—we'll take you another way through the woods. But you will have to pay us."

I had no choice and I gave the man some money.

"That's not enough," he said to me.

"Take my wedding ring," I said and I began to take it off my finger.

"No," a second man protested. "I won't take a woman's wedding ring. It's enough. We have to go."

I thanked Faiga and said good-bye to her. I couldn't believe that Sarah and I were now in the hands of these three men, who looked like bandits and who I didn't think I could trust. But what could I do? We had to go with them. One of the men took my bundle and I carried Sarah as we walked out of the house and through the dark, still-sleeping town.

We walked and walked. They took us on a path through a forest, a path that became narrower the further in we walked. The ground was packed with snow, and I was glad I wore my boots but my feet were still very cold. Sarah had developed a cold again, and she started coughing and sneezing. As we walked, I sang to her and told her stories so she wouldn't be frightened.

At a certain point, the men stopped walking and one of them turned to me.

"The border is just ahead," he whispered. "We don't know where the Russian soldiers might be. You have to be silent. Can you keep the child quiet?"

I nodded and whispered to Sarah. I spoke to her as if she were an adult, not a three-year-old child.

"Sarenka, we must be quiet here. Can you do that? It is very important. I won't talk to you, and you won't talk to me."

She nodded and put her little finger to her lips, to show that she wouldn't speak.

We walked in silence through a snow-covered field. We saw no one and when we entered the woods again, one of the men whispered that we had just crossed the border over into free Lithuania. I breathed a sigh of relief and kissed Sarah again and again.

CHAPTER 9

We continued walking till we came to a small cottage. One of the men told me that his uncle lived there.

"You will have to stay there," he said. "Someone else will take you on to Vilna."

They brought Sarah and me into the house. It was very dark inside and an old man lay on a mattress that was on a wooden platform. He was smoking a black cigarette and coughing between puffs.

"Here are two more, uncle," the man said. "They aren't paying us enough."

The old man kept coughing and then struggled to sit up. Finally, he spoke.

"These damn things are killing me. What did you put inside?" He was speaking to a woman who was standing on the other side of the room.

"You know what's inside," she rudely answered him. "I cut up leaves—you know there's nothing else."

I put Sarah on the floor and without another word I opened my bundle.

"I have something for you, mister," I said, as I searched around for my cigarettes. I located several right away and gave them to him. He took them from my hand, eagerly lit one with shaking fingers, and took a deep draw.

"Ahh!" he said, holding the cigarette between his lips. "Real tobacco. I haven't had any in a long time. Where are you from?"

"I'm from Warsaw."

He took another deep draw of the cigarette.

"My three sons are in the army in Warsaw. They went to fight the Nazis."

"Then they are probably safe," I told him. I didn't want to tell him that they were either dead or in a German prison camp.

"What do you want us to do now?" the nephew asked the old man.

"You go. I'll get..." He started coughing again, and I didn't understand the name he said, but he waved his hand for the three of them to leave.

"You can pay?" he said to me, when he stopped coughing.

"Yes," I answered.

"You'll stay here tonight. In the morning someone will bring you to

Vilna."

Two other women came in from another room and started arguing with the old man. I assumed they were all his daughters-in-law. He told them to make some food, and they grudgingly made boiled potatoes with hot milk. That night, Sarah and I slept on the floor, covered by a blanket that I had in my bundle. The stove gave off only a little heat, and it was very cold in the cottage. Sarah's cold was getting worse, and I was very worried that she would develop a fever.

The next morning, December 6, the old man sent one of his daughters-in-law to get the man who would take us to Vilna. I found my remaining cigarettes and handed them to the old man. He held my hand and kissed it and thanked me for the wonderful gift. Then I offered him some money.

"No, no," he said to me. "You gave me enough. Save what you have for the driver."

One of the women screamed at him, and he told her to shut-up. Then he gave me some advice.

"You and the child are dressed too well. Do you have something else to put on? Put scarves on your head, like our women wear. You don't want to look like you are from Warsaw. Also, don't open your mouth when you are in the wagon. Your Polish is city Polish—they will know you are not from around here."

I found a shawl in my bundle and put it around my head and shoulders. Then I put a scarf over Sarah's head and coat so she looked more like a peasant's child. The old man yelled at one of the women to get an empty bottle from a shelf.

"Hold this empty medicine bottle while you are in the wagon. It will look as if you are going to a doctor."

I thanked the man for his wisdom. He must have done this before for others, and he knew what tricks worked.

Soon the woman came back with a driver and a wagon, and the old man told the driver where to take me. Again, I thanked him for helping us and said good-bye to the three women. They didn't answer, and I left with the driver.

Sarah and I sat in the back of the wagon. It was snowing again, and I covered us with the blanket. The man told us not to talk. There were Lithuanian soldiers everywhere, and it had to look as if we were a local family. I had the empty bottle in my hand, under my blanket, in case we were stopped, but no one bothered us.

The road became busier, and there were now more houses everywhere. Suddenly, the man stopped the wagon in front of a building, got out, and tied the horse to a railing. I saw that we were at a kind of inn, or *kretchma* in Russian, where men gathered to drink vodka.

"You have to pay me now," he said. "I'll be back soon. I'll bring you something too."

"It's very cold out here," I said to him. "And my child is sick."

"I won't be long," he snapped. "Pay me."

So I gave this man the last of my money. Sarah and I huddled together in the wagon while he went inside. Sarah kept sneezing and coughing, and I was increasingly concerned about her.

Finally, after about forty-five minutes, the driver came out, singing a Polish song. When he handed me some sausage, I could smell the vodka on his breath. He got into the front of the wagon, snapped the reins, and we drove on. Soon, I could see that we were approaching the city of Vilna. I started to get very excited and kissed Sarah and whispered to her.

"Look at the big houses! We're in Vilna! We're going to see your *tata*."

I leaned up to the driver and told him to take us to Sadova, 6, the address Father had sent to me. I couldn't believe that we were finally here.

When we came to that building, the driver helped us out of the wagon and handed me my bundle. I think he expected more money. When I didn't give him any more, he spat on the ground and left.

Sadova, 6 was a rooming house. When we rang the bell to go in, a man I knew well from Warsaw, Yossel Mlotek, came to the door. He greeted us warmly and brought us inside.

"How did you get here?" he asked. "Your husband is at the train station, waiting for you. He has been going there for the last few days, hoping you would come!"

"It's a long story," I said to him, "for another time. Can you take us to his room? We are both cold and exhausted and Sarah is sick."

Mlotek took us up to Father's room, and I put Sarah into the bed. A little while later I heard someone running up the stairs, and it was Father. I was so happy that I was shaking. I hadn't seen him since early September, but it felt as if we had been apart for years! Sarah sat up and gave him the hard piece of bread and dried-up flowers that she had been holding for so long.

"It's a present for you," she said shyly, "so you have something to eat."

Father wanted to take her in his arms, but she didn't want to get off

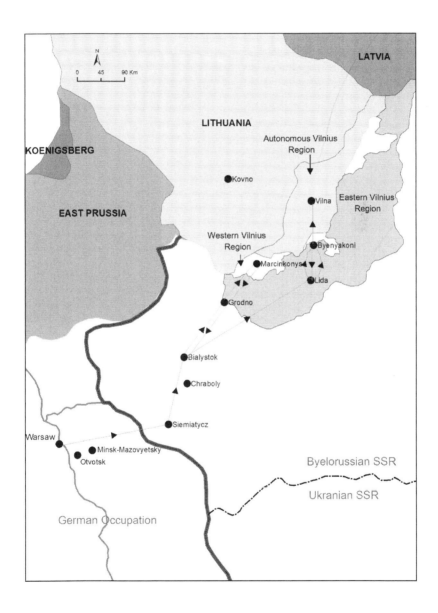

Esther's journey from Warsaw to Vilna

my lap. So we just sat there on the bed, the three of us, together at last after such a long time.

Later, after we had eaten and Sarah went to sleep, I told Father everything that had happened from the time he left Warsaw nearly two months before. He couldn't believe what we went through, and as I told him the stories, I couldn't believe them myself. But all those things had really occurred, and I had gotten Sarah and myself across the borders and to Father in Vilna. Father then told me about his escape from Warsaw.

CHAPTER 10

The day that he left, Father recalled, he had spoken to his friend and colleague Joseph Goldstein, who said that he might leave Warsaw also. But Father told me that he didn't stop off at Goldstein's home because his friend was a procrastinator, and he was afraid he would try to talk him out of going immediately. At any moment, Father said, he was ready to turn back and return to us, and he needed to leave as quickly as he could so his courage and determination wouldn't desert him. He started walking out of the city—there were no trains running at the time. At the outskirts of Warsaw, he waved to a passing truck that stopped for him. The truck was filled with Polish officers and Catholic nuns and some children. He showed the driver and the officers his card from the Writers' Syndicate, and they agreed to give him a ride. When he got on the truck, he took out the block of chocolate I had given him and broke it into pieces for the children and cut the cucumber for the adults.

After many hours, the truck stopped and the soldiers got off. A little while later, the nuns told Father that they were turning off to a side road where their cloister was located, and he couldn't travel any further with them. They said that further down the main road was the town of Chraboly. As he walked towards the town, the sky was black with smoke, and when he got closer he realized that the town was burning. He walked in another direction and came to a railroad track where a train had stopped and he saw people standing there. When he went over to ask if they knew what had happened, he recognized some of the men as Polish and Yiddish journalists from Warsaw! They had taken one of the last trains to leave the capital two days earlier but were stopped because Chraboly and the railroad tracks had been bombed by the Germans. Some soldiers had arrived to help the townspeople and had told the men from the train that they would try to get some military trucks to transport them south.

When the trucks eventually arrived, Father and the writers were driven to a town further east, near the Byelorussian border, where they were brought to an empty school building. The soldiers told a few townspeople that important writers from Warsaw were in that school, and soon people began arriving with food. One of the Jewish writers recognized someone from the town as a fellow Jew. When he told the man that there were Yiddish journalists in the group, the man quickly organized several Jewish families from the town to host all the Jewish writers. It was just before Rosh Hashanah, which would start on September 14 that year, and the Jews of the town couldn't let a *landsman* not have a place to stay and some good food to eat as the Jewish New Year approached.

Father was taken to the home of one of the Jewish families. As they sat down to dinner, the host turned on the radio. The news was terrible—the Germans had arrived in the suburbs of Warsaw and the airplanes were bombing the city. Soon, the announcer said, they were afraid that the tanks would come into the town.

"When I heard that," Father continued, "I couldn't swallow the food I had in my mouth. And I was so afraid for you and Sarenka that I began to cry as I hadn't since I was a boy. When I told my kind hosts why I was crying, they started crying, too."

He stayed with that family for a few days, but each day discussed with the other journalists where they should go. The Polish journalists decided to go south towards Romania, and Father later heard that the Russians had arrested them. The Jewish journalists decided that they would go north and try to get to Vilna in Lithuania. Although the Russians officially occupied Lithuania, Vilna and a large section of the country were technically independent and under Lithuanian control. Vilna also had a very large Jewish population.

"We had walked several miles outside the town when we were stopped by a Soviet patrol. A young Russian captain asked for our identification and we showed him our Polish Writers' Syndicate cards. Then the Russian asked us in Polish, 'Are you Jews?' "

"For a moment none of us said anything. Finally, one man took a chance and said, 'Yes, we are.' "

"Where do you want to go?" asked the captain.

"We want to get to Vilna," Father said he answered.

"Yes," the Russian answered. "It's safer for you people there. I will give you a letter for safe-passage there, and we can take you as far as Bialystok."

Father didn't know until much later that the day before, September 17, the Russians had invaded Eastern Poland as part of their pact with Germany and that area was now under Soviet control. The Russians drove the small group to Bialystok where they stayed until the captain arranged for papers that gave them permission to travel to Vilna by train. Father arrived in Vilna in late September and went to the Yiddish Writers' club. The journalists there told him he could find a room at the boarding house where I later met him, and in a short time he found a position as an editor

Sarah, Esther, and Moshe – Vilna, February 1940

Esther, Sarah, and Moshe – Vilna, December 27, 1940

of one of Vilna's Yiddish newspapers.

The room we were in was in a building Jewish students had used before the war and now housed mostly Yiddish journalists. But it was only for men so we had to leave as soon as possible.

We found a room with a Polish family, but it was too small and too cold so we moved to a larger room that had a big black wood stove in the middle of the room. I was able to cook in that room, and I tried to make it feel like home. We enrolled Sarah in a Jewish nursery school, and she was happy to be able to play with other children. The long, terrible journey was finally behind us.

We were safe, we thought, at least for a time.

CHAPTER 11

In June of 1940, the Soviet Union sent thousands of soldiers into Lithuania and officially annexed the whole country, including the independent area of Vilna. Joseph Stalin said he was "protecting" Lithuania and the Lithuanian president, Antanas Smetona, left the country. On August 4, there was a plebiscite for the people of Lithuania to vote whether or not to become part of the Soviet Union. Of course, it was a phony election. The Russians reported that the people had "overwhelmingly" voted to join them, and the country became known as the Lithuanian Soviet Socialist Republic. So now we were part of the Soviet Union. For a while there was no real change in our daily life.

But that summer, some Polish Jews convinced the Japanese consul, Chiune Sugihara, and the Dutch consul, Jan Zwartendijk, who both resided in the nearby city of Kovno (also known as Kaunas) to issue them exit or transit visas. Without these, it was impossible to leave Lithuania. The Japanese visa showed permission to enter and transit through Japan and the Dutch visa gave a final destination as Curacao in the Caribbean, which didn't require an entry visa. Several thousand Jews got these visas in the summer, and they left Lithuania for Russia and farther east. When we heard about these visas, I told Father we should try to get one and leave Lithuania, but Father thought we were safe where we were.

"We don't know where these visas will take us," he told me. "And it can be dangerous to cross into Russia. Let's stay here in Vilna for now."

But as time went on, I became convinced that we had to leave Lithuania. My sixth sense had told me that Father should leave Warsaw when the Nazis invaded in 1939, and it was now telling me we had to go. Sugihara and Zwartendijk both left in September after their consulates were closed, but they had left blank visa papers behind. Forgers were able to fill out these visas to make them look real. I was determined to get one for my family.

The news we managed to get from Poland was very bad. The Nazis were sending Jews into labor camps. In November 1940, we heard that the Jews in Warsaw were being forced to live in a ghetto. We were unable, however, to find out what had happened to any of our relatives.

Life was also changing for the Jews in Lithuania. Gradually, that fall and winter, the Soviets closed synagogues, Jewish cultural and religious organizations, and almost every Yiddish newspaper, including the one Father worked at. How did we survive? Two big American Jewish charities, the Hebrew Immigrant Aid Society—the HIAS—and the Joint Distribution Committee were still able to help us in Vilna. Then, the Soviets started arresting and deporting Jewish activists, Zionists, writers and intellectuals. Some were even executed in Lithuania. I knew we had to leave.

Our friend the actress Shoshana Kahan, and her husband, Lazar, who had also managed get to Vilna, told us about a man who was forging the exit visas. Soon after the Kahans left Vilna in early 1941, I convinced Father to find that man. We were able to buy an exit visa with our three names on it. The forged visa would allow us to leave Lithuania, enter Russia, and travel east, travel away from Europe, away from Hitler, away from Stalin.

Using money we had been sent by a Jewish writers' group in America, we bought tickets for train passage from Vilna to Moscow and then from Moscow to Vladivostok in the far east of Russia. At the Vilna train station, the Russian border official looked at our Polish identity cards and then at the exit visa with our three names on it. He stamped the visa and wished us a good journey. I couldn't believe it had been that easy. Years later I heard that for some unknown reason, the Russians had allowed Jews with Polish papers who had the Japanese or Dutch visas to leave Lithuania, but they wouldn't allow Jewish Lithuanian nationals to leave. Maybe it was because they considered those Jews Soviet citizens. But at that moment, all I cared about was that Father, Sarah, and I were getting on the train. It was the first week of March 1941.

It took us two days to get to Moscow. We were allowed to stay in that city for four days before boarding the Trans-Siberian Railroad for the trip to Vladivostok. The train ride took nine days. We traveled through Siberia, which was covered with deep winter snow. Everything in the bleak March landscape was white – the snow, the heavy clouds, even the birch trees on both sides of the tracks. Every now and then we passed through very poor villages and saw people bundled up in heavy clothing. Sarah liked to look out the window and wave at the people. Occasionally, they waved back at her. On the sixth day we passed the southern tip of Lake Baikal which completely frozen. It was a very long train ride, but the further away we traveled from Europe, the more relaxed I became. The three of us were together and safe.

When we arrived in Vladivostok, we were told by some Jews already there that in order to go directly to Japan, we had to get permission from the Japanese consul there. But when Father went to the consular office, it

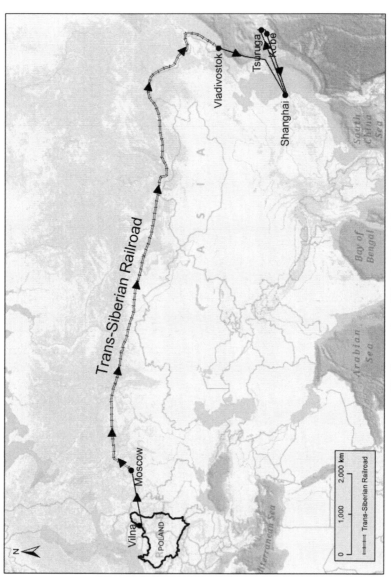

The Journey from Vilna to Shanghai

seemed our luck had run out. He was told that the consul had left Vladivostok two days earlier, and we would have to go to Shanghai, China. Although Shanghai was under Japanese control, there was an area known as the International Settlement that was independent and didn't normally require a visa of any kind to go there. However, the Japanese official said that they were now requiring permits to go to any area of Shanghai and that Father would have to wait for a permit to be sent from Shanghai.

We were terribly disappointed. Some friends had gotten to Japan and from there had obtained visas to Canada and a few even to America, but it seemed that we would have to remain in Russia for a time. We found a room in the Intourist Hotel which was managed by a Russian Jew who was a proud Communist. He also confessed to us that he was a member of the NKVD, the Russian secret police, which we weren't sure was true.

"You should stay here in Russia," he said to us. "Russia is a paradise for Jews."

We didn't think that was true, either, but he was very kind to us and to other Jews who were staying at that hotel. When Passover began on April 11, he managed to find matzohs for us, and we were able to have a seder.

After five weeks, a permit finally arrived from China, and we got permission to travel to Shanghai. Even though the Yiddish Writers' Union in New York had sent us money, we had to travel as cheaply as possible. We got passage on a freighter that was stopping in Shanghai on its way to Singapore for repairs. The ship had only a few passenger cabins. Father slept in the men's cabin while Sarah and I were in the women's cabin. The ship was carrying herring, and the whole boat smelled strongly of fish. By the time we arrived in Shanghai two days later, on May 1, everything and everyone smelled of herring.

When we got off the freighter with our belongings, the Yiddish writer Menachim Flakser was waiting for us at the dock. Father had sent a telegram to a Yiddish writers' group in Shanghai, and they had arranged for Flakser to meet us and take us to a room they had found for us. From the very first, from the earliest time of the war, the Yiddish writers helped one another and did whatever they could to make a terrible situation a little easier. Once again, they were helping us.

Shanghai was like nothing we had experienced. It was hot, crowded, dirty, and smelled of rotting garbage. There were no sewers in most areas and everyone's waste went into the street. And it was, of course, Chinese!

We were European and used to European faces, but here, almost every face was Asian. It took a while to get used to that, to signs that were in

Chinese and that we couldn't read, to rickshaws pulled by barefoot men, and little children urinating on the street. It was a different world!

Our small room was in a very old building with mostly Chinese people, but some Russians and Germans also lived there. We had a small hibachi stove, which I used to cook our food. The day after we arrived Father went to the Japanese consul to get permission to use our visa to travel to Japan, but it was four weeks before we were allowed to go.

In June, we took a boat to Japan. When we came to the port of Tsuruga, we were met by representatives of the Japanese Jewish Committee. They paid for our transportation to Kobe, and they told us that Tadeusz Romer, the ambassador to Japan from the Polish government-in-exile in London, was also trying to help Jews get visas out of Japan. The visas that we and many of the other Jews had stated that we could only remain in Japan for a few weeks. But the central government in Japan had agreed to ignore the expired visas, even the ones they recognized as forgeries, if the Kobe police agreed. A bribe had been paid to the Kobe police, and the Jews were left alone.

There were several thousand Jews in Kobe while we were there, all waiting for a visa to somewhere, anywhere — to Canada, Australia, South America, maybe even the United States. Father visited consulates and embassies, but it was no use. Our good friends the Weingartens had gotten a visa to Canada before we arrived, but we knew others who were still there, waiting as we were now waiting. In 1940 the small Jewish community had established a club, two synagogues, and even a newsletter to try to make the stay in that city easier. The American Joint Distribution Committee made sure we had enough money for food and rent. Truthfully, while we were in Japan we felt more like tourists than refugees. Father, Sarah, and I lived in a very nice boarding house owned by a Chinese man and his Japanese wife. The man had lived in Manchuria so he spoke a little Russian, and we were able to communicate. It was he who told us the news on June 22 that the Nazis had invaded Russia.

Menachem Flakser, who greeted Esther
and Moshe when they first arrived at the
Shanghai dock on May 1, 1941

Passover Seder with members of Yiddish writers group. Seated center with
black dress, Shoshana Kahan. To her right, Yerachmiel Weingarten and his
daughter Jala. To her left, Alex Weingarten and Hanka Weingarten. Kobe,
Japan – April 1941

CHAPTER 12

At first, we couldn't believe that the Germans had broken their pact with Stalin and had invaded the Soviet Union, but it was true. Not only had they attacked Russian-occupied Poland and Russia itself, but Lithuania as well. Had we not left when we did, we would have been in Nazi hands, as were the nearly quarter of a million Jews who lived in Lithuania.

The summer of 1941 was very hot in Kobe. I had never experienced such high, humid temperatures. We and the other Jews kept trying to get visas, to find a country that was willing to accept us, but most of the doors were closed. Romer, the Polish ambassador, still managed to get a few families permission to enter the United States or Canada or other safe countries, but starting in August 1941, the Japanese officials said that all the "refugees" in Kobe could no longer remain in their country.

Do you remember I used to sing a Yiddish song, *Vu Ahin Zol Ich Geyn?* It was written before the war by a Yiddish actor named Korntayer, and I first heard it while we were living in Vilna.

> *Vu ahin zol ich geyn?*
> *Ver ken entfern mir?*
> *Vu ahin zol ich geyn?*
> *'Siz farmacht yeder tir!*

After the war I learned that this song was sung in the ghettos throughout Europe and later in Displaced Persons camps, but even in Japan, Father and I understood the words very well. *Vu ahin zol ich geyn?*

> *Tell me where shall I go*
> *Who can answer my plea?*
> *Tell me where shall I go?*
> *Every door's shut to me!*

The Japanese told us we had to leave. There were about a thousand Jews still left in Kobe. We had to go back to Japanese-occupied Shanghai, to the International Settlement, which didn't require an entry visa. We didn't want to return to that city, but we had no choice.

One day in the early fall, our Japanese landlady knocked on our door.

Esther, Moshe, and Sarah with their Japanese landlady and her daughters - Kobe, Japan - September 9, 1941

"Porando, Porando," she excitedly said to us.

Then she rapidly spoke in Japanese and again said, *"Porando."*

We figured out that *"Porando"* meant Poland, but we couldn't understand what she was saying. When her husband came home, he told us in broken Russian that they had heard that the Japanese government told Romer, the Polish ambassador, that he could no longer stay in Japan. Once he was gone, we felt that we and the rest of the Polish Jews in Kobe might not be safe and that we should leave as soon as possible. With the help of the Joint Distribution Committee, we received money for passage on a ship that would take us back to Shanghai. We left in October, one of the last groups of Jews to leave Japan.

When we were back in Shanghai, the Jewish Committee helped us find a room. This one was also in an old building crowded with Chinese families and refugees like us.

Even though we got a little help from the Jewish organizations and from the wealthy Iraqi Jews who had lived in Shanghai for a long time, life was very hard. Father had to find work, and he did anything he could to earn some money. He wrote advertisements for stores and businesses in any language they needed—Polish, Yiddish, English, Russian, Hebrew, German. He wrote monologues and lyrics for Jewish actors and actresses. The problem was, of course, that these paid very little money, but we did the best we could. Sarah started school at the Shanghai Jewish School, which had been built and paid for by the Iraqi-Jewish Kadoorie family. That family also paid the tuition for any child whose family, like us, couldn't afford the school fees.

In late November, a small miracle happened. The HIAS had been able to arrange for some visas to the United States and the three of us—Father, Sarah, and I—got a visa to go to America on December 11, 1941. But, of course, that never took place.

On December 7, 1941, the Japanese attacked Pearl Harbor in Hawaii. Within days, they occupied the International Settlement and the entire city of Shanghai was under Japanese control. All British and Americans citizens living in Shanghai, including the Iraqi Jews, who were technically British citizens, were interned outside the city. Our American visa was worthless because America was now at war with Japan.

There were more than 20,000 Jews living in Shanghai in 1941. Most, like us, were refugees from Poland and Germany. In the beginning, nothing really changed—the Japanese authorities made no distinction between Jewish and non-Jewish foreigners. Sarah went to school, Father found work wherever he could, and we lived as best as possible in those circumstances. We always made sure Sarah had enough to eat, even if Father and I didn't. If there was an egg, Sarah needed to have it. Yet even though life was very hard, we were happy that the three of us were together. We had old friends from Poland and Lithuania in Shanghai, and we made new friends. There were Jewish clubs, Jewish newspapers, and Jewish theater. On the floor of our room, Father drew advertisements for the Russian-Jewish Club, and he made New Year's cards that he sold before Rosh Hashanah. He was the assistant editor of a small weekly Jewish publication. He arranged Yiddish vaudeville shows and was the master of ceremonies at plays and concerts.

Once, he wrote a satire about Hitler. In order for the play to be presented in public, he had to submit his Yiddish script, in English translation, to the Japanese censors. He changed most of the words so it was just a comedy about life in Europe. When he gave the actors the Yiddish script, he also gave them masks he had made that depicted Hitler, Mussolini, Goebbels, and others.

Cast of the production of Sholom Aleichem's play *The Two Hundred Thousand* - Center (in long dress): Shoshana Kahan, 4th from right: Moshe. Shanghai Jewish Club - November 21, 1942

"Are you crazy?" said one of the actors when he read the script and saw his mask. "The Japanese will arrest you when they see the play! They will arrest all of us!"

"Don't worry," Father told him. "The censors approved the script."

On the night of the play, the whole audience knew that they were going to see a satire about the Nazis, and there was a lot of nervous whispering before the curtain went up. At the rear of the theater were two Japanese soldiers who didn't understand a word of Yiddish. When the audience started to laugh, the Japanese also laughed. They didn't seem to recognize who the masks represented, and they thought they were seeing a comedy in a language they didn't know. The play was a big success.

The Shanghai Jewish School that Sarah attended was run as if it were part of the British school system. I think it followed a curriculum from Cambridge, England. In addition to those studies, Sarah had Jewish and Hebrew classes, and she also had to learn Chinese. Sarah learned English very quickly in that school, which was on a very high level, and she received a very good education there.

Like Japan, the climate was very different than it was in Eastern

Europe. The winters were cold and damp with a lot of rain, and the summers were very hot with high humidity. In the summer, anything that I washed would take days to dry. The water wasn't clean and I had to boil it for a long time on the small hibachi stove so we could drink it and cook with it. We had to cook all our vegetables, even our fruit, when we could afford it, because raw food would make us sick. We also had to get injections so we wouldn't get cholera or typhoid, but many of our friends and neighbors became sick with various diseases.

Towards the end of 1942, we heard a rumor that the Japanese, probably under pressure from the Germans, would be ordering everyone who arrived in Shanghai after 1937 to move to a "Designated Area for Stateless Refugees." In essence, the Japanese would force recently arrived Jews like us to live in a ghetto. The following spring, notices went up telling us "stateless refugees" that we had to move our homes and businesses to an area known as Hongkew. Hongkew was a very poor, crowded section, maybe a square mile in size, and thousands of Chinese lived there. The order said that we had to move there by May 15. Although it never had a wall or a fence, it was patrolled by Japanese soldiers, and you needed to get a pass to go out of the area. It was possible to get these passes, but you had to wait in line for a long time to get one.

A Japanese general named Kanoh Ghoya, a very short man, was in charge of the Hongkew ghetto, and he called himself "The King of the Jews." If he was giving out the passes, he would sometimes slap a Jew in the face for no reason at all. If the person didn't move or react, General Ghoya would smile and give them the pass. But at other times, he gave candy to children, and he allowed the children to go to school outside the ghetto. He was a very unpredictable man, and we were nervous about what he might do to make our lives more difficult. I sometimes wondered if he knew that his last name meant a "gentile woman" in Yiddish.

After the war, we heard about how terrible it was for our family and friends, for all the Jews, in the Warsaw, Vilna, and other ghettos. Looking back I can only say that in our Shanghai ghetto we lived an almost normal life, considering that there was a war going on. Father, Sarah, and I were together in a small room, there was no bathroom or toilet there, but we managed. Sarah continued going to school, Father did whatever work he could find, and there was occasional money from Jewish organizations. We lived among the Chinese, but we never heard anything from them against us. I bought what I could from the Chinese pushcart peddlers on the street, and they were all friendly to us. Never, while we lived in China, did we feel any anti-Semitism from the Chinese, and even the Japanese didn't close our schools, newspapers, restaurants, or meeting places. We weren't afraid that there would be a knock on the door in the middle of the night and we would be taken away.

In 1944, the Americans started bombing Shanghai. It was terrifying for all of us—the air raid sirens reminded me of the bombing of Warsaw in 1939 and Sarah often couldn't sleep because she thought the bombers would come. When the siren sounded, Father and I had agreed that I would take the briefcase with our important papers, he would take Sarah, and we would go to the cellar of the building, which was used as the bomb shelter. But usually, when it sounded, I grabbed Sarah and started running down the stairs.

In June of 1944, we heard about the Allies landing in France. Much of the accurate news about the war we found out in secret, from people who had illegal short wave radios and heard the news from England or America. Father and I began to hope that the war would end soon. But the Germans remained in control in Poland, and we could get no news about our family there. The reports about the Allies' successes in Europe made us optimistic, and after we heard about a very big victory for the Americans and English in January 1944, Father and I made an important decision—we decided to try to have another child. Even though we were still under occupation, we believed that Japan would lose, and we would all be freed. In early April, I found out that I was pregnant.

The end of the war in Europe came in May with the unconditional surrender of the Germans. We also heard that Hitler had committed suicide. We—and all the Jews in Shanghai—were jubilant, but we had to celebrate privately and quietly. The Japanese had been German allies, and they were still at war with the Americans and British. And the bombings still continued.

The ghetto itself didn't get bombed until the middle of July. Bombs destroyed some buildings in Hongkew, and many Chinese and Jews were either killed or injured and hundreds became homeless. We had such mixed feelings about the bombings! We wanted the Japanese to lose the war, we wanted the allies to win, but we were afraid the bombs might kill or injure more of us. It was a very frightening time for everyone, yet we were hopeful the war would soon end, and we were excited about having another child.

It was from our friends who had the illegal short wave radios that we heard that the United States dropped new kinds of bomb called atomic bombs on the Japanese cities of Hiroshima and Nagasaki on July 6 and 9,

1945. A few days later, Japan surrendered, and the Americans and British troops came in and liberated Shanghai and all of occupied China. The war, the long terrible war, was finally over.

CHAPTER 13

One day, just after the war ended, Father and I were talking about what to name our baby when it was born.

"If it's boy, I'd like to name him Pinchas, after my father," I told him, "and since Sarah is named after both our mothers, I think we should name a girl Victoria."

Father agreed with me. Sarah also liked our choice of names, though she told us she only wanted a sister.

Gradually, in the coming weeks, we began to hear the horrible news from Poland, from Lithuania, from Germany, from all of Europe. Millions, millions, of our people had been murdered by the Nazis. The labor camps we had heard about were really concentration camps, death camps, crematoriums. We tried desperately to find out about our sisters, brothers, all our relatives and friends, and slowly we heard that most of them had died, either in the ghettos or the camps.

You, Judy, were born at the Shanghai Jewish Hospital on October 16, 1945. We named you Judith, after the heroine from the Bible, not Victoria. We couldn't name you after any of our sisters because we weren't yet sure who had lived and who had been killed, but we wouldn't name you Victoria. For the Jews, there had been no victory.

Some Jewish organizations started helping us get information about our relatives and let us notify them that we were also alive. That is how we found out that my brother Samuel, who was living in Paris, was the only one in my family who had survived. He had been in a concentration camp where his wife and children were killed. My sisters and their families—they were all dead, all murdered by the Nazis either in the Warsaw Ghetto or the camps. Father had lost three brothers and their families, but his one sister Rivka and her husband Isaac were alive. They survived in Belgium, where they lived, because Isaac was a tailor at a German factory and was a "protected" worker. They didn't keep their two daughters with them because they were always afraid the Nazis might at any time deport or kill all of them, so their girls lived under false names in a Catholic convent school where the nuns protected them. The girls had to pretend to be Catholics. When the war ended and the family was reunited, the younger daughter, Sara, who was the same age as our Sarah, no longer remembered that she was really Jewish. She had a very hard time being a Jew again and not a Catholic.

Sarah holding Judy - Shanghai, November 1945

Judy and Sarah - Shanghai, 1946

I had visited Rivka and Isaac in Belgium in August 1938 and it was the first time I had ever been out of Poland. Sarah and I had taken a train from Warsaw to Brussels and we had to travel through Nazi occupied Germany. Just before we left, I had gotten my passport but for the first time in my married life, I made a mistake and signed with my maiden name, Brodowicz, instead of Elbaum. Father delicately scraped off the signature with a razor blade and I re-signed my name. Each time I went through passport control at a border, especially in Germany, I was afraid that someone would notice the alteration and arrest me. Fortunately, nothing happened.

Two of Father's nieces survived—Shaindle, who later went to Canada and her sister, Esther Malka, who went to Israel. They were the only two remaining from his eldest brother Yossel who was killed in 1942. But all the others, from Warsaw, from Minsk-Mazovyetsky, from Lodz where Father had family, my cousin Rahel who had taken me and Sarah to the bus when I tried to leave Warsaw—all had either died of disease or hunger in the ghettos or been killed in the concentration camps. All had been murdered by the Nazis. Each day we and all the other Jews in Shanghai found out more about what had happened to our people in Europe and how few of our relatives were still alive.

Just before you were born, we moved out of the Hongkew area and got a slightly better room at 630 Muirhead Road. Taking care of a new baby was not easy in Shanghai. I couldn't just wash the diapers—I had to boil them on the small stove, but because they didn't dry quickly in Shanghai's humid climate, I needed to iron them. Even though I nursed you, for any additional milk, I had to buy canned Carnation milk, because the local milk might be contaminated. Of course, I had to make all the baby food each day because we didn't have a refrigerator.

On January 1, 1946, the American Embassy opened in Shanghai, and we and most of the more than 20,000 Jews in the city tried to get visas. But it was very difficult to secure permission—the Americans, it seemed didn't want us either. Even though Jewish agencies like the HIAS and the Joint said that they would sponsor us and we wouldn't "become a burden" to the Americans, as some in the U.S. thought, the government said that the sponsor couldn't be an organization. It had to be an individual. And so again, we waited, we waited to have a place to go. *Vu ahin zol ich geyn?* Tell me where shall I go?

Clockwise: Esther, Moshe's brother Akiva Elbaum, Akiva's wife Roiza, Isaac Kirsch, Moishe's sister Rivka Kirsch, Akiva and Roiza's daughter Marie, Rivka and Isaac's daughters Sara (Suzanne) and Janine Kirsch, Sarah, and Akiva's daughter with his first wife (Chana) Fanny - Brussels, Belgium – August 1938. Akiva, Roiza, Fanny, and Marie were killed in Auschwitz.

Isaac, Rivka, Janine, and Sara Kirsch – Belgium - August 1946

Moshe's niece Shaindle Neumark with her daughters Klara and Miriam, and her husband Shlomo – Wrozlov, Poland - July 8, 1947

Slowly, people began getting visas to Canada, Australia, Argentina, Brazil, and finally, to America. The ardent Zionists wanted to go to Palestine but the State of Israel didn't yet exist. Palestine was a British mandate and they weren't letting in any Jews. Later, our friends the Tukachinskis, whose son, Joseph, went to school with Sarah, managed to get to Israel. Joseph, who changed his name to Yosef Tekoa, became the Israeli ambassador to the United Nations.

Shoshana and Lazar Kahan were among the first to get American visas. Just before they left, they both developed typhus. Shoshana recovered but Lazar died. But before he died, they were informed that their two grown sons, who had also escaped Warsaw, had been killed somewhere in the Soviet-occupied area. Their daughter, Lily, had managed to survive in a very clever way. Lily was a singer and was in Italy when the war broke out. Like all passports in those days, her Polish passport had her name, Lily Kahan, hand-written in ink, not typed. She made a dot above the hump of the 'h' so that it looked like an 'l' and an 'i' and her name became Lily *Kalian*. She lived safely as a Polish woman in Vatican City for the rest of the war and stayed on in Italy as Lily Kalian.

Shoshana left for America as soon as she recovered and told us she would try to help us get visas.

We did the best we could. Sarah continued at the Shanghai Jewish School, I took care of you and our small room, and Father wrote, made advertisements, and found odd jobs. As the Jewish community diminished, it became harder for him to find work and we were grateful that the HIAS helped us a little.

An interesting thing happened to Father one day when he took a train from Shanghai to nearby city to do some work for a Russian printer. He was sitting in the crowded second-class car, reading a Yiddish newspaper, when he noticed an old Chinese man staring at him. Finally, the man came over to him, spoke to him rapidly in Chinese, and pointed repeatedly to the newspaper and then to himself.

"I understood a few of the words he was saying," Father later said to me, "and one word that he kept repeating was, *youtai*, which means Jewish in Chinese. I then realized that he saw the Hebrew letters on my newspaper. He didn't know the words were in Yiddish, he only recognized the letters, and he was telling me that he was Jewish. He was a Chinese Jew, probably one of the few remaining from the small community of Chinese Jews in the city of Kaifeng!"

We had heard about these Chinese Jews but had never met any in Shanghai.

"What did you say to him?" I asked Father

"Basically, we kept smiling at each other and I told him my name and said I was a writer. He said *youtai* a few times and I repeated *youtai*. And before I got off the train, I offered him the newspaper and he was so happy to take it. I was sure he couldn't read any of the words, but he knew that alphabet. He shook my hand many times when I got to my stop and waved to me from the window."

I think today there are no more Chinese in Kaifeng who consider themselves Jewish. That man was probably one of the last.

On Mother's Day in 1947, I received a wonderful present from Father and Sarah. There was no money for flowers or chocolates so Father wrote a song for me, using the melody of *Besame Mucho*, a song that had become very popular, and that Father and I loved. The morning of Mother's Day they both sang the song to me in Yiddish.

> *L'omir hynt bahzingen di mameh—*
> *Di shaynsteh, di besteh, di kleegsteh in the gantzeh velt...*
>
> Let us, today, serenade Mother—
> The prettiest, best, and smartest in the whole world...

Until Father died, he always bought me something for Mother's Day, but that song, written by him and sung to me by him and Sarah in our small room in Shanghai, was one of the best gifts I ever got. Often, I still sing it to myself and I remember that moment as if it were yesterday.

Good news finally came to us in February 1948. Rabbi Chaim Walkin, who left Shanghai with his family in 1947, was able to secure a sponsor for us. He and other respected Jews and Jewish organizations were asking prominent Jewish families in the United States to help refugees get visas. They only needed to be the official sponsors—the HIAS and the Joint Distribution Committee would bear any financial responsibility. Rabbi Walkin had convinced Stephen Klein, who owned Barton's Chocolates in New York, to sponsor many Shanghai Jews. We were among those who were then able to get visas to America. In March 1948, after six and a half years in China, we left Shanghai.

We took an American freighter with room for passengers because it was the least expensive way to travel. We had bought two large carved camphor-wood chests while we were in Shanghai, and we put everything we owned, except for the clothes we would need on the ship, into those chests. Father put each chest into a wooden crate and nailed the top down. The four of us had one cabin on the ship, and we ate in the ship's small dining room.

The first morning at breakfast, eggs, bread, cheese and other food was put on the table.

"Don't eat the eggs," I whispered to Sarah, Father, and you, as I pointed to the hard-boiled eggs. "There's something wrong with them. And don't eat that bread, either. Take a hard roll."

The next morning, the same breakfast was on the table, and I asked one of the other passengers why the Americans bleached their eggs and their bread. She started laughing.

"They don't bleach them! Why do you think they do?"

I pointed to the white eggs and the white bread.

"They are white," I told her. "There must be something wrong with them."

That was the day I understood that everything, including food, was going to be different in America. In Poland, Lithuania, Japan, China, everywhere we had ever been, eggs were brown, and bread was dark. Even in children's books, eggs were pictured as brown. We had never imagined that eggs could be white! And the white bread on the table, that we started calling *vatteh broit*—cotton bread—that was the Wonder Bread Americans

Sarah, Esther, Judy, and Moshe – Shanghai 1947

liked.

The freighter stopped in Hong Kong and Manila and then crossed the Pacific to San Francisco. On April 20, 1948, we arrived in America. After eight and a half years of wandering, with forty American dollars in our pockets, we finally found a home.

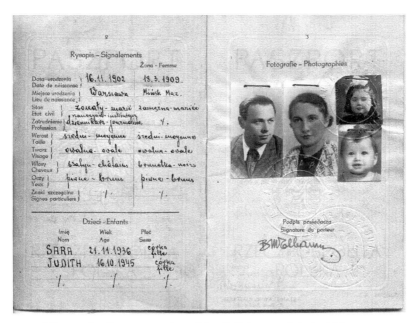

Elbaum family passport issued by Polish consulate in China - January 8, 1948

Moshe and Esther's U.S. visas and U.S. entry stamps

CHAPTER 14

I had some distant relatives from my mother's side who lived in San Francisco and when we had written to them before we left China, they invited us to stay with them.

We got off the freighter at the pier and waited on the immigration and customs line. We saw that the customs official, a big, muscled man in a uniform, was making everyone open their suitcases and boxes and looking inside.

"I don't know what we will do," Father said to me. "I can't open these crates without something to pry open the nails, and I have nothing."

You, Judy, were two and a half years old, and you had climbed on top of one of the crates. Just as the official came over to us, you started singing *God Bless America*, a song Sarah had taught you on the ship. Everyone, including the customs official, stood still and listened till you finished. Then the man smiled, stamped our papers and said,

"Welcome to America."

We stayed in San Francisco for about ten days. The relatives I had never met before were wonderful to us. We thought the city was the most beautiful we had ever seen. It was so clean and bright compared to Shanghai, and in April the weather was cool and sunny. All the buildings in the city looked new, which they were, since most had been built after the earthquake.

Did I ever tell you I had an uncle who was in San Francisco during the 1906 earthquake? My mother had a brother who wanted adventure, so he left Poland and came to the United States a few weeks before the earthquake. He was so frightened by the quake, he wrote to my mother, that his hair turned white overnight. I don't think that was really true, but that was the story in my family. He then decided America was too dangerous for him, so he went to France, joined the French Foreign Legion, and was killed in World War I.

I loved San Francisco. I loved giving you a bath in a tub that had hot water that I didn't have to heat on a stove. I loved walking on the hilly streets of the city with you and Father and Sarah and not having crowds of people around us. I loved looking at the store windows even though we didn't have the money to buy anything.

Sarah holding Judy – San Francisco,
April 1948

Judy and Sarah on the train from San Francisco to New
York – May 1, 1948.

We left for New York by train and several days later were greeted at the station by a very good friend from Poland, the actor and singer Menashe Oppenheim. He took us to an apartment on Prospect Place in Brooklyn that Rabbi Walkin and his wife had rented for us and we began our new life in New York. The best part was that Father had a job waiting for him as a journalist for the Yiddish newspaper *Der Morgen Zhurnal—The Morning Journal*.

We spent the first few months getting used to Brooklyn, learning to ride the subway, going to Prospect Park near our house, becoming reacquainted with old friends who had also survived, and learning about America. In September, even though she was only eleven and a half years old, Sarah started high school. Academically, she was on the level of American ninth graders.

There was one thing though, that we hadn't expected at the high school. During the first week, there was a fire drill and the loud ringing of the bells terrified her. It reminded her of the sirens in Shanghai, and she thought they were going to be bombed! For the first few months, whenever there was going to be a fire drill, a counselor took Sarah into her office so she wouldn't be scared.

Our apartment on Prospect Place had only one bedroom. As soon as we could afford it, we moved to a larger apartment on St. John's Place. You, Judy, started kindergarten at the Jewish Kinneret School when you were four years old. The principal of that school was Yerachmiel Weingarten, our friend who was able to leave Kobe for Canada just before we arrived there and who later immigrated to New York. He and his wife and children became some of our closest friends.

In 1953, The Morning Journal merged with another Yiddish newspaper, *Der Tug—The Day*—and Father lost his job. That time was very hard for us financially. But a year later, he started working as the city editor of *Der Forvertz—The Jewish Daily Forward*—and he was there, as editor and columnist, until he died. At *The Forward* he worked side by side with Isaac Bashevis Singer and Eli Weisel, who both wrote for the paper in the 1950s and '60s.

For a few summers, I worked as a cook in small Catskill summer resorts. One summer Father and I rented a guesthouse. We renamed it "The Little Club Hotel," and Father painted that name on a green and white sign that hung near the road. I cooked the meals and ran the guesthouse during the week and Father came up on weekends. Unfortunately, the guests were mostly our friends, and since Father gave them discounts, we didn't make a

Esther, Moshe, Sarah, and Judy – The Catskills(?) – New York, Summer 1949.

profit. Eventually, I got a job outside the home, for the first time since I was a kindergarten teacher before I got married. The company I worked for in Manhattan, Yardney, made special types of batteries. I didn't like leaving you as a latchkey child but I needed to help earn money for our family.

During those early years in America, just after the war, we heard more and more reports about what happened to our relatives and friends, to the Jews of Europe at the hands of the Nazis and their collaborators and sympathizers. Some Jews we knew didn't want to hear about it anymore, didn't want to talk about it, didn't want to tell their children. But Father and I believed that we had to know and had to read about and talk about what had happened, and that you and your sister also had to know. If people stopped telling the story, Father kept repeating in columns, then the world would forget. Even at a joyful time, at our seders, you read Binim Heller's poem *In Varshever Ghetto* about the start of the uprising in the Warsaw Ghetto, which began on the first night of Passover. You still read it now.

In the small city where I had been born and raised, Minsk-Mazovyetsky, the ghetto the Jews had been forced into was liquidated in 1942, and most of the Jews there, including my dear sister Tsesha and her family, were sent to the Treblinka concentration camp. A few hundred remained in a nearby labor camp. On January 10, 1943, those people were going to be sent to Treblinka, but some of them managed to run away and took refuge in the Kopernik School on Siennicka Street. When they saw the Germans coming, they threw stones and bricks at them. So the Nazis set fire to the school and burned them alive—220 people. The few surviving Jews of that city witnessed what happened from hiding places.

A few years before his death, Father was the director and host of a performance in New York of the poetry and songs of the well-known Yiddish writer Mordechai Gebirtig, who was murdered by the Germans, together with his wife and two daughters, in Poland in 1942. One of his most famous songs, which he actually wrote before the war, was *Es Brent*. Do you remember, it? I used to hum it or sing it to myself.

> *Es brent, briderlekh, es brent!*
> *Oy, undzer orem shtetl, nebekh, brent!*
>
> *On fire, brothers, it's on fire!*
> *Oh, our poor little village is on fire*

When I was told about the Jews being burned alive in the school in my home town, it was that song that I thought of - *Es brent, briderlekh, es brent!*

This was one story, one story out of thousands—really, one story out of millions.

But we also heard stories of bravery, of Christians who saved Jewish lives, even when they put themselves in danger.

My friend Basha Nuss, in whose house Sarah and I stayed two nights before we left Warsaw, was saved, together with her mother and sisters, by a Polish man named Stefan Gajewski. After the war, Basha married Stefan

Left to right: Sarah, Esther, Judy, Stefan Gajewsky, Moshe, Basha Nuss Gajewsky (Esther's friend from Warsaw), and Yolanda Gajewsky - New York, 1951

and they came to America a few years after us.

While we were living on St. John's Place, a young Jewish family moved onto our floor. The husband, Gary Frydman, was a Holocaust survivor but his wife, Dorothy, was a Canadian from Hamilton, Ontario. In 1954, Dorothy had a little boy, and her mother came to stay with her for a while to help with the new baby. When her mother, Mrs. Stiglick, returned to Hamilton, she mentioned to her neighbor, a recent refugee from Poland, that she left her daughter with an easy heart. A wonderful woman named Esther, she told her, who was also a Polish refugee, lived on her floor and was helping her and Gary with the baby. Esther was married to a prominent Yiddish journalist who had also been a writer in Poland.

One day, Dorothy knocked on my door.

"Can you come into my apartment, Mrs. Elbaum?" she asked when I answered the door. "My mother is calling from Canada, and she needs to ask you something."

When I picked up the phone, Mrs. Stiglick was talking to someone in the background.

"Esther," she said excitedly in Yiddish, "I had forgotten your last name and I just asked Dorothy and told it to my neighbor. She wants to know if your husband's first name is Moshe and if you lived in Warsaw."

"Yes," I told her, "It is Moshe and we did live there. What is going on?"

"Just a second. There is someone who wants to talk to you."

"Esterka?" a woman yelled in Polish, "This is Yadja!"

I started to scream. Yadja Lederman was my second cousin. I had been certain she had died in the war, because I had heard nothing about her. Not only were we cousins, but because we were close in age, we had been very good friends. I couldn't believe this was true. We were both yelling and crying and laughing on the phone, not knowing where to begin our stories.

A few weeks later, I took a bus to Hamilton and was reunited with the cousin whom I hadn't seen or heard from since 1939. While we were together, we told each other about our lives since we last were together. Mostly, we cried.

Yadja, I knew, had been married before the war, but she and her husband both developed typhus. Yadja recovered, but her husband of just nine months died. In 1940, her brother, Jerzy, was put onto a train that they found out later was going to Auschwitz, and they believed that he had been killed there.

"Then they forced us all to move into the Warsaw Ghetto," Yadja told me, "and Renya and I were there until they sent us to a labor camp."

Renya, her sister, was thirteen years younger and still a teenager when they were sent away.

Miraculously, both survived the labor camp and while at the camp, Yadja met her second husband, Leo Lieberman, and Renya met her husband, Henry Haran.

"After we were liberated, we didn't want to go back to Warsaw. No one was there anymore, no one was alive. So the four of us ended up in Walbrzych—the Germans called it Waldenburg—in the southwest of Poland not far from the Czech border."

"How long did you stay there?" I asked her

"Not long. Leo and I wanted to get out of Poland as quickly as we could. We ended up in a Displaced Persons camp in Admont, Austria and waited for a visa of any kind to get out of Europe. Our son Archie was born in the camp in 1946. Finally, the Stiglicks, who we didn't know, sponsored us and we got a visa to Canada. We arrived in 1948 and they were just wonderful to our family. Sammy was born here in Hamilton in 1951."

"The same thing happened to us," I told her. "We were sponsored by the Kleins, who we had never met, and still haven't met, though we thanked them by letter when we arrived in America. And where are Renya

Yadja, Leo, Sam, and Archie Lieberman – Hamilton, Ontario, 1952.

and her husband now?"

"Unfortunately, they and their daughter Alina are still in Walbrzych, in Poland. Because of the communist government there, it's impossible to get them a visa. They think we don't try to help them, but we do. The Poles just won't let them out."

"And Jerzy? You said he was alive?"

"Yes, it was unbelievable," Yadja cried. "While we were in Walbrzych we received a letter from an organization that was helping survivors find each other. He had contacted them, and they found me and sent me the photo he had sent them, with a message on the back. He said he was alive and living in France and gave us his address. We had been certain that he had been killed in Auschwitz."

My visit to my cousin in Hamilton was too short, but it was wonderful for me to reunite with someone in my family and meet her husband and two boys. It wasn't until several years later that Renya, Henry, and Alina were finally allowed to leave Poland, but the Polish government would only let them out if they went to Israel. It was another few years till they finally came to Canada. And it wasn't till 1965 that Jerzy came to see them in Hamilton. They hadn't seen each other for twenty-five years. That's why, whenever there is a wedding or a Bar or Bat Mitzvah we always travel to one another's *simchas*—there are so few of us who lived, we have to be together to celebrate joyful occasions.

CHAPTER 15

What shall I tell you now? You know the rest. Sarah got married to Herbie Goldenberg in 1957, and Father's sister, Rivka, who lived in Belgium, and my brother, Samuel, who lived in France, both came to the wedding. Father had seen his sister when he went to Europe two years earlier, but I hadn't seen my brother in more than twenty years. It was an overwhelming reunion for us. He had been in a concentration camp where his wife and children had been killed. He remarried after the war and had a son, Serge. Having them at Sarah's wedding was a very special gift for all of us.

Father, you, and I moved to Queens from Brooklyn in 1960, and I stopped working for Yardney when the company moved to Connecticut. You married your first husband in 1966. Sarah and Herbie had four sons and now have grandchildren. They all called me *baba.*

We had a full life in New York, though we never had a lot of money. We had many wonderful friends, both old and new, and you know how I loved to give parties! Whether for a holiday or just to have people at our home, I enjoyed cooking and entertaining. So many actors, actresses, musicians, and writers from the Yiddish world in New York came to our home—Mina Bern, Ben Bonus, the Liebgolds, the Boziks, and of course, Shoshana—all of them were part of our social life. Goldstein and Nudelman were very close to us—remember, they had been witnesses at our wedding. Both of them had lost their families in the Holocaust, but they remarried and Nudelman had children with his second wife. Father and I often went to the Yiddish and English theater, and in addition to his work at *The Forward,* Father started doing news commentary during Sunday's *The Forward Hour* on WEVD radio.

In January, 1969, your Father, my beloved husband Moshele, died of a heart attack. He was only sixty-six years old. He had had a heart attack two years earlier, but we thought he had recovered. His death was a terrible shock to me, to all of us. Just a few weeks before, we were walking together on the street when an elderly couple walked by us, arm in arm. I remember thinking that that was how I imagined Father and me when we were very old—walking together on the street, arm in arm. But it wasn't to be. I was alone.

Moshe and his sister Rivka Kirsch at their reunion - Brussels, Belgium - 1955

Esther's brother Shlomo Brodowicz with Moshe's sister Rivka - New York, December 1957

Esther – New York, 1957

From left: Adam Burstyn, Moishe Nudelman, Shimon Dzigan, Ann Burstyn, Israel Schumacher, Joseph Goldstein and Moshe. Nudelman and Goldstein were witnesses at Esther and Moshe's wedding. Dzigan and Schumacher were a Yiddish comedy team. New York, 1964

Moshe during broadcast of the *The Forward Hour* - WEVD Radio - New York, February 1968

Those years were very hard for me. I had to learn how to be by myself, even how to write checks and pay the bills. Father had been a very traditional European husband and had always handled our family's finances. Even when I was working, he had been in charge of the money. Now, at age 59, I had to begin balancing a checkbook, paying the rent, and trying to live on my own.

But life changes and life goes on. You gave birth to Rina in 1970, but your marriage was not going well, and you divorced when she was just one year old. Because you started teaching again, I became Rina's babysitter and this was a wonderful development for me. I adored my granddaughter—the first after four grandsons—and it gave me such pleasure to be able to spend time with her and watch her grow. And I was happy to be able to help you at that time of your life. But another big life change happened to me, one I never expected.

In 1972, I took a trip to Israel to visit old friends. One of the people I went to see was Yerachmiel Weingarten. Yerachmiel and his wife, Hanka, had retired and moved to Israel where his son, Alex, and his family lived, but some months before I visited him, Hanka had died. Both of them had been our very good friends in Warsaw and then New York. You remember that not only was he your principal at the Kinneret School, but for many, many years, the first Passover seder was at the Weingartens' house and the second seder was at our house. That's the reason having a second seder became a tradition for us.

Yerachmiel and I had a common history. We had both escaped from Poland and followed the same route to Kobe, Japan. We had many mutual friends and knew each other's children. We were very comfortable together. Before I returned to the United States, I promised him that I would return to Israel for an extended stay to see if I would want to emigrate there and marry him.

In the meantime, you met Gary and the two of you planned to get married in the fall of 1973. I went back to Israel for six weeks in the spring of 1973. While I was there, Yerachmiel and I decided we would marry and I would move to Israel. We got married when he came to the U.S. in September. He needed to return to Israel because he was in the middle of writing a book about the Polish-Jewish children's author and pediatrician Janusz Korczak. I remained in my apartment in Queens to get ready for my big move and to be at your wedding.

I had many mixed emotions while I was packing. I had to go through all of Father's books and papers and decide what to do with them. Some things I had already donated to the YIVO Institute for Jewish Research, but there were still many documents, not only from the years in America, but also from China and Lithuania. Sorting through them was hard because memories kept flooding back. In the end, I gave everything to the YIVO and kept only a few of his personal items and, of course, photographs.

You and Gary had your beautiful wedding in October. I was able to leave you and move so far away only because I knew that you and Rina and Gary would be a happy family together. Sarah and Herbie and their four boys were going to make *aliyah* and move to Israel that following spring so half my family would soon be there, too. In December 1973, I did what I never imagined I would do. I left my home in New York and moved to Tel Aviv, Israel.

Again, I had to adjust to a new life. I loved Israel, and I could get by with English and even Yiddish, but I started going to class to learn Hebrew. It was difficult for me. Perhaps it was my age, but I never really became proficient in the language. Yerachmiel had a lovely apartment in a beautiful neighborhood in Tel Aviv, and I quickly learned how to live in that city. And having Alex and his family nearby, and later Sarah and her family in Haifa, made us both very happy. Yerachmiel and I were contented to be with each other.

We visited the United States when your daughter Lauren was born and then again when Yerachmiel was trying to get an American publisher for his book. You sent Rina to us when she was just six years old, and it was a delight for all of us to have her there. We were at your house in New Jersey at the end of September 1979, when Gary returned from the supermarket on Sunday morning with an armload of *New York Times* newspapers.

"It's in there," he announced as he put the papers on the kitchen table. The two of you started looking through the paper and then reading an article in one of the sections.

Then you turned to me.

"Sit down, Mom," you said. "I want you to read something."

In the New Jersey section of *The Times*, September 30, 1979, was an article you wrote about me to commemorate the recent fortieth anniversary of the Nazi's attack on Poland. It was titled "A Woman of Courage," and it told the story of my leaving Poland and my journey to Lithuania, Japan, China and ultimately, the United States. I could barely read the words because my eyes kept filling with tears. I was so proud that you had an article published in *The New York Times*, and I knew that Father would have been proud of you, too. But mostly, my tears were because I realized

**Esther and Yerachmiel Weingarten- Tel Aviv,
August 1981**

that you had listened when I told you the stories, that you had heard me. I now knew that what had happened to me, to all of us, would not be forgotten. From that day on, I carried a copy of that article in my handbag.

Each time we went back to Israel, it was hard for me to leave you, Gary, and the girls. I never knew when I would see you again, and I missed you all very much. All of you came to Israel in the summer of 1981, yet as soon as you left I couldn't wait to see you again.

One day in 1982, Yerachmiel went to the post office to mail some letters. When he didn't return after an hour, I became concerned. I then received a telephone call that he had collapsed on the street and had been taken to the hospital. By the time I got there, I was told that he had died. He had had a massive heart attack, and they couldn't revive him.

I was a widow again. Again, I had to learn how to live alone. But I decided to remain in Israel because it had become my home, and it was more economical for me to live there. My journey has taken me to many different countries, and I don't want to move any more.

You wanted to hear my story from beginning to end. Did I remember everything correctly? I don't know for certain, but I think so. My story is like a tree with large branches that lead to little branches. Every incident reminds me of another, which reminds me of still another. My memories are always with me and for me, in my thoughts, the war has never ended. When you write this some day, remember to say that I loved all of you very much. You said I was courageous in your article—I don't know if I really was, but I can tell you that I did the best I could. Always, I did the best I could.

Esther at her 80th birthday party – New York, December 1990

POSTSCRIPT

My mother died in Israel on October 29, 1998. She was 87 years old.

When I first listened to my mother's tapes, I was impressed by the names, dates, and events that she remembered after more than fifty years. But after crosschecking what she told me on World War II historical websites, encyclopedia entries, calendars, and other sources, I was astonished that her recollections were so accurate about everything. One website that was particularly helpful was the Museum of Jewish Heritage's *JewishGen Shtetl Seeker*. When I typed the name of a town as I heard my mother say it, the site prompted me to use the "Daitch-Mokotoff Soundex," which gave many possible spellings to towns that phonetically sounded like that. It then gave the exact location of those towns, which enabled me to pinpoint the places my mother was talking about. In every case, the town was exactly where she said it was. Her memory was amazing.

In 2003, I attended a screening of a documentary film, *Shanghai Ghetto,* which told the story of five German Jews who had lived in Shanghai during the war. At the end of the film, there was a question and answer session with the two producers, Dana Janklowicz-Mann and Amir Mann. One man in the audience asked a question that at first I thought irrelevant. But that question—and its answer—changed my whole understanding of my parents' lives in Japan and China. It, in essence, clarified the reasons for the Japanese government's rather benign treatment of the Jews and illuminated the amazing saga of the Jews' survival in Shanghai.

The questioner asked, "Do you think that what Jacob Schiff did for the Japanese in 1904 had an influence on how they treated the Jews in Shanghai?"

Amir Mann answered, "Yes. We are fairly certain that it did."

I was puzzled. I had never heard of Jacob Schiff or what he did. I later spoke to Mr. Mann privately and he briefly outlined the story. But further research gave me the full account of the remarkable association between a German-Jewish financier in New York and late Meiji-era Japan—and how it helped the Jews thirty-five years later.

Schiff was born in Germany in 1847 to a distinguished rabbinical family but worked for banking and brokerage companies. He came to New York after the Civil War and in 1874 began working for the German-Jewish banking house of Kuhn, Loeb and Company. In 1875 he married the daughter of Solomon Loeb, one of the founders of the firm, and in 1885, became the head of the company.

In 1904, Japan was fighting Russia in the Russo-Japanese War. They had waged war with China just ten years earlier and their treasury was depleted. Japan asked for loans from various European banks, but those bankers were certain Russia would beat Japan and didn't want to risk losing their money. Jacob Schiff, however, agreed to lend Japan more than $200 million at very favorable rates. This wasn't done for financial reasons—he couldn't be assured that he would ever be paid back. Schiff saw this as a way of exacting revenge on Tsarist Russia, which was becoming increasingly anti-Semitic and had recently allowed a horrific pogrom against the Jews in the city of Kishinev. During the three days of rioting, hundreds of Jews were killed or injured and most of the Jewish homes and businesses were destroyed.

Schiff's money financed the war and enabled Japan to defeat Imperial Russia. The subsequent Treaty of Portsmouth was a huge victory for Japan—it gained control over Korea, Formosa, parts of Manchuria, as well as other areas of the Far East. After the war, Schiff became a hero in Japan and was the first foreigner to be awarded the Order of the Rising Sun by the Emperor. The Japanese didn't quite understand what it meant to "be Jewish" and knew little about Jewish customs and practices, but they believed Jews were "wealthy, powerful, and smart," and they were indebted to a Jew. And the Japanese have very long memories.

I now understood why the Japanese honored visas to their country that they knew to be false, why they allowed Jews to stay on even after those visas expired, and why they were "left alone," as my mother recounted, in Kobe.

How the Jews were treated in Shanghai was surely the greatest legacy of Japan's indebtedness to a Jew. Though they eventually succumbed to German pressure to start a ghetto, it was a ghetto where Jews lived among the Chinese, a porous ghetto where children went to school, restaurants were open, synagogues were allowed, and no trains were leaving for concentration camps. Neither of my parents knew about Jacob Schiff and his role in this chapter of the story.

Over the years, I have been invited to speak to Holocaust classes about my family's experiences during the war. I developed presentations for middle school, high-school, and university students, as well as for adult audiences. I begin all my presentations by recounting an incident that occurred when I was eleven years old. My father had taken me to an exhibit of Holocaust photographs at the Jewish Museum in New York and before we left, he bought us both small brass pins of the Hebrew word *zachor* — remember.

As we were walking towards the subway, I complained to my father.

"Why do you take me to these exhibits? Why are you always talking about the war, and the Nazis, and Shanghai?"

My father stopped walking and pointed to the pin he had put on my coat.

"Look at what this pin says. It says *zachor*—remember. If I don't teach you, and you don't teach your children and others about what happened to our people, then the world will forget."

I didn't understand his lesson then, when I was eleven years old, but I remembered it later, when I started listening to my mother's stories, when I started hearing what she recounted, and when I started telling others about it.

I was invited to speak to sixth-grade classes because the language arts curriculum in the public schools of Northern Nevada, where I now live, includes a unit on heroes, with one chapter about the Japanese consul Chiune Suguhara, who issued those Japanese visas. Often, when I asked for questions, a student would invariably ask me if I still had that pin my father gave me.

"No," I would answer, "I didn't really understand its meaning, and I lost it long ago."

One evening at my synagogue, I was speaking to my friend Martha Gould when I saw that she was wearing a little Hebrew *zachor* pin on her lapel. I couldn't believe it.

"Martha! Where on earth did you get that pin? I talk about it at all my presentations!"

When I told her about the one I had had, she took off her pin and gave it to me.

"Take it. I'll get another. There is a Holocaust survivor in Las Vegas whose name is Ben Lesser. He started the Zachor Foundation to give out these pins. Call him—I'm sure you can get more."

When I contacted Ben Lesser, he told me that he, too, had gotten a pin in the 1950s and decided several years ago to have them made so that he could give them to people when he spoke about his Holocaust experiences. He charges no money for them and had so far given out more than forty thousand pins. I ordered several hundred and started giving them out at the

**Judith Elbaum Schumer giving a presentation
about her family – Reno, NV, 2012**

end of my presentations. I always thank the students for letting me speak to them because they are helping me do what my parents wanted me to do. They are helping me to *zachor*, to remember, and to tell the story to others. In their "Thank you" letters to me, many of students assure me that they, too, will *zachor*.

I sometimes play the cassette tapes I made with my mother. I hear her voice tell me all the stories about her life and her journey of survival. She was a remarkable woman and I am grateful that before she died, she knew that her story would be remembered. She knew that I had listened. She knew that I had heard. And she knew that she wouldn't be forgotten.

THE FIVE POSTCARDS

On the next pages are five postcards that my father, Moshe Elbaum, sent to his brother-in-law Isaac Kirsch (and sister Rivka) in Belgium during the war. They follow my family's route from Vladivostok to China, then to Japan and back again to China. They were written in German since they were being sent to Nazi-occupied Belgium. (Note the round Nazi "stamp" on 4 of the postcards.) My aunt and her family had kept them all these years and her granddaughters sent copies to me in April 2012.

Isaac and Rivka were able to remain in their apartment in Brussels during the war because Isaac worked as a tailor for a company that was controlled by the Germans and he and my aunt were "protected." That is surely why they were allowed to send and receive mail during the war. Their daughters Janine and Sara (Suzanne) were hidden in a Catholic convent with false papers under the names of Janine and Suzy Dekerke.

My friend Eleonore Jaksztait of Reno translated the postcards from German to English.

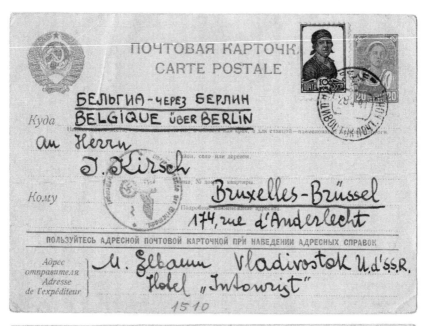

ПОЧТОВАЯ КАРТОЧКА
CARTE POSTALE

БЕЛЬГИА - через БЕРЛИН
BELGIQUE über BERLIN

Куда

An Herrn

J. Kirsch

Кому

Bruxelles-Brüssel
174, rue d'Anderlecht

ПОЛЬЗУЙТЕСЬ АДРЕСНОЙ ПОЧТОВОЙ КАРТОЧКОЙ ПРИ НАВЕДЕНИИ АДРЕСНЫХ СПРАВОК

Адрес
отправителя
Adresse
de l'expéditeur

M. Elbaum Vladivostok U.d'S.S.R.
Hotel „Intourist"

1510

Vladivostok, d. 12/XI 41

Unseren Theueren!

Ihr habt gewiss erhalten alle
Unsere Briefe und wisst schon
über Unsere Reise, interesante
Reise. Es ist aber eingetreten
eine zeitweilige Änderung, da
wir fahren nicht über Japan,
sondern über Shanghai, wo
wir werden bleiben einige
Monate und wohnen in die
Amerikanische Konzession. Wir
haben schon bekommen
die nötige Permits mit Wohn=
recht. Wir werden an Euch
regelmässig schreiben, aber
schreibet Ihr oft an Uns, an Herr
hängig von Briefbekommen...
Wir sind gesund, Grüsse u. Küsse
Sonia, Esther, Mordche

Schreibt! Unser adresse: HICEM SHANGHAI

Vladivostok, USSR   date: 12/IV-41
(April 12, 1941)

Our dearest!
   I believe that you have already gotten our letters and you know about our big, interesting trip. But in the meantime there was a change in plans - we will travel to Japan - but we have to travel through Shanghai - we will stay there for a few months and live in the American concession. We have gotten the necessary permits with permission to live there. We will write to you in a short time. But please write often to us, even if you don't get our letters.
   We are healthy. Greetings and kisses,
   Sara, Ester, Mosche

Write! Our address: **HICEM SHANGHAI**

(Note: HICEM was an acronym of the merger of three Jewish migration associations: New York-based HIAS (Hebrew Immigrant Aid Society); ICA (Jewish Colonization Association), and Emigdirect, a migration organization based in Berlin.)

片信明政

Exp:
M. Selman
c/o Hicem P.O.Box 1925
Shanghai

BELGIQUE
VIA GERMANY

Mr.
J. Hirsz
Bruxelles-Brüssel
174, rue d'Anderlecht

Shanghai 6/I-41

Unsere Teueren!
Endlich sind wir schon in Shanghai, auf dem mit- u. unseres nach Amerika. Wir bleiben hier jedenfalls einige Monate. Wir sind glücklich, dass wir schon sind außer die gefahr zu senden nach sybir verschickt.

Wir sind gesund und Füllen sich gut. Im einen nächsten Brief werden wir Euch aus-führlich schreiben gegen unser Reise War, wo und alles genau. Unser Sareuka ist Wunderschön abgereist, Sie war die einzige, die auf die schiffkraukheit nicht gelitten hat Tränen! Schreibt an uns, aber sofort, weil ein Brief dauerte über 4 wochen wir 2 küssen Euch son Estera, Ша

Shanghai 6/V-41
(May 6, 1941)

Our dearest!
Finally, we arrived in Shanghai on our detour to America. We will stay here for a couple of months. We are happy that we are no longer in danger of being sent to Siberia.

We are healthy and we feel very good. In the next letter we will tell you more details about our trip, why we had to do the detour. Our Sarenka is wonderfully tanned and she was the only one who didn't get seasick. Dearest, write to us right now because one letter takes longer than four weeks.

With kisses, your Sara, Estera, Moi.

(Note: After the Soviets occupied Lithuania in June 1940, many Jewish writers and intellectuals were deported to Siberia. Some were executed. Even in Vladivostok, there was probably danger of being sent to Siberia.)

CARTE POSTALE

Adresse

BELGIQUE
via U.S.A.

MR
J. Kirsch

BRUXELLES

174, rue d'ANDERLECHT

B.M.ELBAUM
KOBE (Japan)
c/o JEWCOM

1323

Kobe – Japan, 15/VII 41

Unsere Teuere!

Vorige Woche haben wir erhalten Eure Postkarte nach Shanghai.. Wie Du selbst Isaak haben wir ja gut getan, dass wir sind von dort abgereist. Wir sind schon jetzt in Japan, in der wunderwollen Stadt Kobe. Wir sind alle gesund. Wahrscheinlich werden wir ja nach Amerika fahren, eventuel nach Canada. Alles ist auf den guten weg. Ihr habt gewiss gedacht über uns wie ihr hatt erfahren wegen der kühner geen. Wir hatten schon zeit gehabt für Euch Packeten mitt Reis und Tee – ja es ist unmöglich worden etwas zu senden.

Teuere! Wir hoffen doch dass wir werden Euch kürzlich kämen sehen und alles erzählen in Freude.

Viele Grüsse und Küsse –
Basenka, Ester, Morris

Kobe, Japan, 15/VII-41
(July 7, 1941)

Our dearest!
Last week we received your postcard that was sent from Shanghai. You can see, Isaak, that it was good that we left. We are already in Japan in the wonderful city of Kobe. We are all healthy. Probably, we will travel to America or eventually to Canada. Everything goes well. You probably were thinking of us when you got the information about the Vilna Goen. We had time to make packages of rice and tea but it was getting impossible to send them.
Dearest! We hope that we will see you in a short time and we can tell you everything in happiness.
Hearty greetings and kisses- Sarenka, Ester, Moisz

(Note: This post card contains a cryptic message, obviously because my father knew it would be read by Nazi censors. The Vilna Gaon ("genius") was an 18th century rabbinic 'sage' in Vilna. When Germany broke its pact with Russia and invaded the USSR, including Lithuania, on June 22, 1941, thousands of Jews in Vilna and the country were executed in the first few days. The genocide rate of Jews in Lithuania (95-97%) was one of the highest in Europe, primarily due to the widespread cooperation of Lithuanians with the Nazi authorities. By July 7th my father must have heard about the occupation of Vilna and may have heard about the beginning of the extermination of the Jews there.

JEWCOM – on the return address– was the Jewish Community of Kobe.)

Shanghai, date 1/XI-41
(November 1, 1941)

Our dearest!
We received all your postcards and we answered every one of them. We are healthy and feel very good but if we weren't so worried about all our relatives everything would be excellent. We were in Japan in the months of July, August and September, in Kobe, and in Yokohama and Tokyo. We should have been able to leave Japan but there are some difficulties and we have to stay here and wait. It shouldn't take too long. From Motele and the children we received no letters. From Josele nothing. We are happy when we receive postcards. It doesn't matter how long it takes. We beg you write often, write often. We also beg you to stay strong and overcome these hard times because it will get better. We kiss you. We kiss you our dearest and hug you against our hearts. Sarenka is already a big girl. On the 21st of November she will be 5 years old. She is wonderful.
Yours, Sara, Ester, Mojs.

(Note: By this date, my father's brothers Motele and Josele (Yossel), with most of their family members, had already been sent to concentration camps where they were murdered.)

Shanghai. The Bund

Shanghai, 28.X.42

Unsere Teuerste!
Wir sind gesund. Fühlen sich
ausgezeichnet. Erhalten Eier
Nachricht durch den Roten
Kreuz in Genève. Bitte schreibt
an uns wie wir sind warm
Ihr kennt. Wir wünschen
Euch alle ein glückliches
Neues Jahr lechaims!

M. ELBAUM, SHANGHAI (CHINA)
c/o HICEM, P.O. BOX 1425

116/252830

BELGIQUE

6789

MR
I. KIRSCH

BRUXELLES
BRÜSSEL

174, RUE d'ANDERLECHT
863

Shanghai, 28.X.42
(October 28, 1942)

Our dearest!
We are healthy. We feel great. We received your letters through the Red Cross in Geneva. Please write to us whenever you can. We wish all of you a Happy New Year lechejrus!
Moses, Estera, Sara Elbaum

(Note: *Lecherjus* is the Polish spelling of the Hebrew/Yiddish word "lecherut" which means "to liberty" and is used in a prayer at Rosh Hashanah, the Jewish New Year: *Teka bashofar gadol lecheruteinu!* - Let the great *shofar* (ram's horn) proclaim our liberation! Its cryptic meaning here – in October of 1942 - is especially poignant.)

Made in the USA
San Bernardino, CA
19 March 2013